BIBLE IQ

1,000 QUESTIONS TO RATE YOUR SCRIPTURAL SAVVY

BY RAYBURN W. RAY

BARBOUR
PUBLISHING, INC.
Uhrichsville, Ohio

© 2000 by Barbour Publishing, Inc.

ISBN 1-57748-837-7

Unless otherwise noted, Scripture quotations are taken from
the King James Version of the Bible.

Scripture quotations marked NIV are taken from the HOLY BIBLE,
NEW INTERNATIONAL VERSION®. NIV®. Copyright © 1973, 1978,
1984 by International Bible Society. Used by permission of
Zondervan Publishing House. All rights reserved.

Scripture quotations marked NKJV are taken from the NEW KING
JAMES VERSION. Copyright © 1979, 1980, 1982 by Thomas Nelson,
Inc. Used by permission. All rights reserved.

Published by Barbour Publishing, Inc., P. O. Box 719, Uhrichsville,
Ohio 44683 http://www.barbourbooks.com

Member of the
Evangelical Christian
Publishers Association

Printed in the United States of America

ACKNOWLEDGMENTS

The author wishes to thank the following family members and friends who made valuable contributions to the preparation of this manuscript: to my wife, Rose Ann, who made useful suggestions on composition and patiently endured my preoccupation with this project; to our daughter, Jennifer, our son, Daniel, and friends, George Knight and John Ishee, who offered encouragement and helped me prepare my first manuscript on a computer.

Finally, I'm indebted to Barbour Publishing for their confidence in this project and to senior editor Susan Schlabach for her helpful suggestions. For the readers, my prayer is that this book will help increase their knowledge of the Scriptures and bless their lives as its compilation has blessed mine.

CONTENTS

INTRODUCTION

Bible IQ was designed to offer lovers of Bible trivia and other serious Bible students a systematic—but fun!—method of testing scriptural knowledge. Rather than using random questions such as those employed in most books of Bible trivia, *Bible IQ* provides one hundred categories of ten questions each, spanning the entire Bible from Genesis to Revelation.

For example, forty-four categories deal mainly with Bible characters, at least twenty categories concern issues of daily Christian living, and twenty or more center on Jesus—His birth, ministry, death, resurrection, intercession, and Second Coming. Other categories deal with major Bible events or basic doctrines.

All should be interesting, fun, and we hope, a challenge to you to further study of the Bible. It is not only the world's best-selling Book, but the world's *best* Book!

Rayburn Ray
Nashville, Tennessee

HOW TO USE *BIBLE IQ*

You can use *Bible IQ* all by yourself, or challenge Bible classes, youth groups, or family members to an IQ contest! The format lends itself to "Category Challenges," in which a person or group challenges another to compete in a given category or categories. For example, the challenge could be on creation, Noah, Solomon, Paul's missionary journeys, family values, or workplace ethics. The index of *Bible IQ* quiz topics found on pages 5–9 makes it easy to locate subjects of interest. Answers by category, with scriptural references, begin on page 217.

HOW TO SCORE *BIBLE IQ*

While some categories will be less difficult than others because of familiarity or special interest, we suggest a uniform system of scoring as follows:

Nine to ten correct answers:	*Outstanding*
Seven to eight correct answers:	*Very good*
Five to six correct answers:	*Fair*
Four or fewer correct answers:	*More study needed*

Scorers are encouraged to accept answers that are essentially correct, remembering that Bible students use various Bible translations that vary in language. The King James Version has been used in most direct quotations, but the New King James Version (NKJV) and New International Version (NIV) and other newer translations have been consulted in cases where the King James was unclear. Blanks have been provided for completion questions, but students and scorers should recognize that various versions may suggest more or fewer words. In presenting the answers, paraphrases or indirect quotes are often used in the interest of clarity or conserving space.

In cases where the King James carries an archaic or obscure answer, a slash may be used in the answer section, giving an acceptable answer from a newer version. For example, the Hebrew children had a diet of pulse/vegetables; Peter resurrected a woman who was called by two names in the same passage: Dorcas/Tabitha. Ground rules should be adopted for the scoring of questions with more than one answer. Enjoy your journey through the Bible!

1

DAYS OF CREATION

1. COMPLETE: "In the beginning _____ created the heaven and the earth."

2. According to the Gospel of John, who participated in creation along with the Father?

3. Who moved upon the face of a dark and formless world?

4. COMPLETE: After separating land and water, the Creator called the land _____ and the water _____.

5. What did God call the two "great lights" that separated day from night?

6. After God created sea monsters and all manner of birds, what did God command them to do?

17

7. COMPLETE: After creating man in His image, God assigned man _____ over all He had created.

8. God finished creation in _____ days and rested on the _____ day.

9. Where did God place man after he was created?

10. What reason did God give for creating a companion for Adam?

SCORE: _____

2

THE FIRST FAMILY

1. What was Adam's occupation while he lived in Eden?

2. Why was Eve called "woman"?

3. CHOICE: Who first tasted the forbidden fruit in Eden?
   a. Adam   b. The serpent   c. Eve

4. What did God place at the garden's east entrance to prevent the first family's return?

5. COMPLETE: Cain's occupation was _____, and Abel was a _____.

6. How did Cain respond when God inquired, "Where is Abel thy brother?"

7. What son of Adam and Eve did Eve regard as a replacement for Abel?

8. What penalty did God promise anyone who killed Cain?

9. Which son of Cain had a city named for him?

10. COMPLETE: "For as in Adam all die, even so in _____ shall all be made alive."

SCORE: _____

3

NOAH AND HIS ARK

1. COMPLETE: In contrast to the wickedness of his generation, "Noah walked _____."

2. Who were the three sons of Noah?

3. After instructing Noah to build an ark, God established what covenant with him?

4. COMPLETE: Noah was instructed to bring _____ of every living thing into the ark, both _____ and _____.

5. After Noah, his family, and the preserved animals were safely in the ark, rain fell for how many days and nights?

6. After 150 days, the ark rested upon what mountains?

7. A dove released by Noah returned with what in her mouth to indicate she had found dry land?

8. After Noah left the ark, what was his first recorded action?

9. What covenant did God establish with Noah after he left the ark?

10. Which son of Noah exposed his father's nakedness, resulting in a curse upon his son?

SCORE: _____

4

ABRAHAM, GOD'S SOJOURNER

1. What was Abraham's name before God changed it?

2. COMPLETE: Abraham's father was named

   _____.

3. Abraham and Sarah migrated from Ur in southern Mesopotamia to what place in Canaan?

4. COMPLETE: Abraham obeyed God's call to leave Haran for a "land _____."

5. What was the covenant that God made with Abraham as he was leaving Haran?

6. Why did Abraham and his family change course and go south into Egypt?

7. Why did Abraham say he misrepresented Sarah as his sister to Pharaoh?

8. Where did Lot choose to live when he and Abraham separated?

9. Abraham begged God to spare what city for the benefit of fifty righteous persons living there?

10. What substitute sacrifice did God provide when Abraham was told to harm Isaac?

SCORE: _____

5

JACOB AND ESAU

1. Who were the parents of Jacob and Esau?

2. COMPLETE: Esau was a skilled hunter, and Jacob was a quiet man who lived _____.

3. What did Jacob use to purchase Esau's birthright?

4. When Esau realized Jacob had stolen their father's blessing, what did Esau resolve to do when their father died?

5. COMPLETE: After Jacob served Laban for seven years to marry Rachel, Laban gave him his daughter _____ instead.

6. What was the new name given to Jacob after he wrestled with an angel at Jabbok?

7. CHOICE: When Jacob met Esau in east Jordan, they:
   a. Declared war   c. Spoke harshly
   b. Embraced

8. Name Jacob's two sons born to Rachel.

9. Jacob and Esau reunited to bury their father
   _____.

10. COMPLETE: Jacob is regarded as the father of the Israelites, and Esau is considered the father of the _____.

SCORE: _____

6

JOSEPH AND HIS BROTHERS

1. Who were Joseph's parents?

2. Why did Jacob love Joseph more than his other children?

3. Which of Joseph's brothers urged that his life be spared?

4. Where was Joseph taken by the traders who removed him from the pit?

5. How did Joseph's brothers try to deceive their father about Joseph's disappearance?

6. How did Joseph answer the seductive advances of Potiphar's wife?

7. Joseph impressed Pharaoh by interpreting his dream that seven years of plenty would be followed by what?

8. What did Joseph put in the sacks of grain purchased by his brothers in Egypt?

9. Which brother was held hostage in Egypt until Benjamin arrived?

10. What did Jacob say upon being reunited with Joseph at Goshen?

SCORE: _____

7

MOSES, AARON, AND MIRIAM

1. COMPLETE: Moses, Aaron, and Miriam were the children of Amram and _____.

2. Who discovered baby Moses hidden in the bulrushes of the Nile?

3. Whom did Miriam enlist as a nurse for the newly adopted baby Moses?

4. Why was Moses given that name by his adoptive mother?

5. Why did Moses slay an Egyptian?

6. COMPLETE: Moses married _____, daughter of the priest of Midian.

7. Why did God appoint Aaron as spokesman for Moses?

8. Why was Miriam stricken with leprosy in the wilderness?

9. What did Aaron do that highly displeased God while Moses tarried at Mt. Sinai?

10. After what occasion did Miriam lead a procession of praise to God?

SCORE: _____

8

FROM THE BURNING BUSH TO THE RED SEA

1. What was Moses doing when God spoke to him in the flaming bush?

2. Why did God tell Moses to remove his shoes?

3. By what name did God identify Himself to Moses when He called him to deliver the Israelites?

4. What excuse did Moses give God for his reluctance to be a deliverer in Egypt?

5. What was Pharaoh's response when Moses asked him to let the Hebrews have a feast in the wilderness?

6. What was the first of the ten plagues visited upon Pharaoh for keeping the Hebrews in bondage?

7. What did the Israelites do to avoid the death of their firstborn sons when the death angel visited Egypt?

8. Why did the Israelites not use leavening in their bread as they left Egypt?

9. What provision did God make for the Israelites to travel safely both day and night?

10. What happened to Pharaoh's army that pursued the Israelites into the Red Sea?

SCORE: _____

9

WILDERNESS WANDERINGS

1. How many years did the Israelites spend in the desert before settling in Canaan?

2. Who advised Moses to select capable leaders to help him counsel the people and settle disputes?

3. COMPLETE: After the Israelites complained about lack of food, God provided _____ in the morning and _____ in the evening.

4. Who held up Moses' hands at Rephidim while Joshua battled the Amalekites?

5. What covenant did God make with Israel as Moses met God on Mt. Sinai?

6. What is the first of the Ten Commandments God delivered to Moses?

7. How many spies were chosen to explore the land of Canaan?

8. Who were the two spies who gave a favorable report of Canaan?

9. Why did God send fiery serpents to plague the Israelites?

10. While not permitted to enter Canaan, Moses viewed the Promised Land from what mountain?

SCORE: _____

10

JOSHUA AND CALEB

1. How did Joshua and Caleb's report of Canaan differ from that of the other ten spies?

2. By what action did Moses designate Joshua as his successor?

3. Whose household was saved in the siege of Jericho by displaying a red cord from a window?

4. What sign indicated the people should follow the priests across Jordan at Jericho?

5. In crossing the Jordan at Jericho, what was the significance of the twelve memorial stones taken from the river?

6. How did the man with the sword identify himself when Joshua approached him at Jericho?

7. What happened when Joshua's men and the priests marched around Jericho seven times and shouted?

8. What did Joshua ask the Lord to do in order to have more time to defeat the Amorites?

9. What land was Caleb given as an inheritance for his faithfulness?

10. What was Joshua's testimony when he charged the people in his farewell address: "Choose you this day whom ye will serve"?

SCORE: _____

11

GIDEON AND THE MIDIANITES

1. Why were the Israelites delivered into the hands of the Midianites?

2. What did the angel who appeared to Gideon at the winepress say to him?

3. COMPLETE: The Lord ordered Gideon to destroy the altar of Baal and replace it with an altar to _____.

4. What confirmation of his call to service did Gideon request from God?

5. Why did God order Gideon to reduce his army?

6. What procedure was used for reducing Gideon's army to 300 men?

7. What three items were placed in the hands of Gideon's soldiers for the assault on the Midianites?

8. Why did Gideon refuse to be made king after his victory over the Midianites?

9. What did Gideon carve out of the gold earrings taken from the Midianites?

10. COMPLETE: Gideon had _____ sons because "he had many wives."

SCORE: _____

12

SAMSON AND THE PHILISTINES

1. According to Judges, why were the Philistines allowed to rule Israel for forty years?

2. COMPLETE: Samson's birth was prophesied by an angel, and his mother was told he would be dedicated as a _____.

3. How did young Samson demonstrate his strength while going through the vineyard at Timnath?

4. What did Samson do when the Philistines solved his riddle about honey and the lion?

5. How did Samson destroy the fields of the Philistines?

6. How did Samson kill a thousand men at Lehi after being bound?

7. How did God quench Samson's thirst after the victory at Lehi?

8. How was Delilah able to cut Samson's hair and deprive him of his strength?

9. After Samson was captured and blinded, what job did the Philistines give him at Gaza?

10. How did Samson kill the Philistine rulers and a large number of celebrants honoring their god Dagon?

SCORE: _____

13

RUTH, NAOMI, AND BOAZ

1. Why did Naomi and Elimelech leave Bethlehem to settle in Moab?

2. What family occurrences prompted Naomi to return to Bethlehem?

3. Name Naomi's daughter-in-law who returned to her home in Moab.

4. How did Ruth answer Naomi when Naomi urged her to return to her home?

5. Why did Naomi ask the people of Bethlehem to call her "Mara"?

6. Who owned the barley field where Ruth gleaned?

7. How did Ruth show her interest in Boaz at the threshing floor?

8. Why did the kinsman nearest to Elimelech decline to redeem Elimelech's land?

9. COMPLETE: Obed, the son of Ruth and Boaz, became the father of Jesse and the grandfather of _____.

10. COMPLETE: As the great-grandparents of David, Ruth and Boaz became ancestors of
_____.

SCORE: _____

14

SAMUEL CROWNER OF KINGS

1. Why did Hannah give Samuel that name?

2. COMPLETE: In gratitude for Samuel, his mother told Eli the priest, "As long as he liveth he shall _____."

3. What did the Lord reveal to Samuel about the future of Eli's family?

4. While Samuel was praying, what did God do to confuse the Philistines who were attacking Israel at Mizpah?

5. What was Saul looking for when he met Samuel for the first time?

6. Why was Saul reluctant for Samuel to anoint him as king of Israel?

7. What sign did Samuel say would be evidence that the people were wrong to ask for a king?

8. How many sons of Jesse were examined before young David was located and anointed king?

9. COMPLETE: As a judge, Samuel traveled from place to place to _____.

10. Who succeeded Samuel as judge of Israel?

SCORE: _____

15

SAUL, ISRAEL'S FIRST KING

1. COMPLETE: Saul's father was _____, a wealthy man from the tribe of Benjamin.

2. Who anointed Saul as king by pouring oil on his head and kissing him?

3. What did God give Saul after he was anointed king?

4. Where did the children of Israel assemble to receive Saul as king?

5. Whom was Saul preparing to battle when he offered an unauthorized sacrifice at Gilgal?

6. What was Saul's great sin after defeating the Amalekites?

7. How did Saul seek relief when an evil spirit tormented him?

8. What son of Saul became young David's close friend?

9. What chant of women celebrating David's victory over Goliath angered King Saul?

10. Who was Saul's daughter who married David?

SCORE: _____

16

THE SHEPHERD BOY
WHO BECAME KING

1. Why was David absent when Samuel first examined the sons of Jesse?

2. COMPLETE: To soothe King Saul's troubled spirit, David was chosen as the king's _____.

3. Why was David confident he could defeat the Philistine giant Goliath?

4. What weapons did David use to kill Goliath?

5. After David's success in battles, what did Saul do to him in a jealous rage?

6. What condition did David meet in order to marry Saul's daughter?

7. How did Jonathan inform David that Saul intended to harm him?

8. What evidence did David produce that he had spared Saul's life in the cave at Engedi?

9. Whom did David marry after Nabal of Carmel died of a stroke?

10. Where was David anointed king of Judah after the death of Saul?

SCORE: _____

17

KING DAVID OF ISRAEL

1. After being crowned king in Hebron, David defeated the Jebusites and made what city his capital?

2. What sign did God give David as a signal to attack the Philistines at Rephaim Valley?

3. Why did David interrupt his pilgrimage to return the ark of the covenant to Jerusalem?

4. COMPLETE: Nathan told David God would not permit him to build the temple, but his kingdom would _____.

5. Why was David moved to show kindness to Mephibosheth, grandson of King Saul?

6. What did Nathan tell David his punishment would be for taking Bathsheba and having Uriah killed?

7. What were David's words when the child born to Bathsheba died?

8. Which son of David killed Amnon for raping his half sister, Tamar, David's daughter?

9. How was Absalom killed during his rebellion against David?

10. How did David secure the throne for Solomon at Gihon Springs?

SCORE: _____

18

KING SOLOMON'S WISDOM AND FOLLY

1. Who was Solomon's mother?

2. Who was Solomon's half brother who tried to usurp the throne and was ultimately executed by Solomon?

3. What did God promise Solomon in addition to wisdom, wealth, and honor if he obeyed the Lord?

4. What counsel did Solomon give two women in a child custody dispute to test them?

5. Whom did Solomon enlist to provide lumber and other supplies for construction of the temple?

6. How did Solomon provide labor for temple construction?

7. What famous visitor from Arabia was impressed with Solomon's wisdom and brought gifts to him?

8. Why was God displeased with Solomon's marriages to foreign wives?

9. Solomon tried to kill a top official he regarded as a rival of his son Rehoboam for the throne. Who was he?

10. A prolific writer, Solomon is considered the primary author of which Bible books?

SCORE: _____

19

KING AHAB
AND JEZEBEL

1. As king of Israel, Ahab ruled in what place?

2. COMPLETE: Ahab offended God by marrying Jezebel and by building a
_____.

3. How did Ahab greet the prophet Elijah when he called on the king during an extended drought?

4. Who hid a hundred prophets in caves to prevent them from being killed by Jezebel?

5. What happened to Ahab's prophets of Baal after they were defeated on Mt. Carmel?

6. What was Jezebel's angry message to Elijah after her prophets were tragically defeated?

7. What judgment did Ahab bring on himself for taking possession of Naboth's vineyard?

8. What penalty did the prophet Micaiah suffer for telling Ahab he would be killed at Ramoth-Gilead?

9. After King Ahab died in battle, how was Elijah's tragic prophesy fulfilled?

10. How did Jezebel die at the hands of Jehu?

SCORE: _____

20

ELIJAH AND ELISHA

1. How was Elijah miraculously fed at the brook Cherith while fleeing from King Ahab?

2. What did Elijah promise the widow at Zarephath who fed him from her handful of meal?

3. Whom did Elijah revive from the dead at the home of the widow in Zarephath?

4. What charge did Elijah bring against King Ahab in the third year of the drought?

5. How did the crowd on Mt. Carmel respond when fire from heaven fell and devoured the sacrifice?

6. After the victory at Mt. Carmel, what did Elijah's servant report after seven trips to view the sea?

7. How did God reassure Elijah in the wilderness when he told the Lord, "I am the only prophet left"?

8. What symbolic act did Elijah carry out to indicate Elisha should be his successor?

9. What did Elisha do to indicate acceptance of his new role as Elijah's successor?

10. What did Elisha request of Elijah as that prophet was preparing to be taken to heaven in a whirlwind?

SCORE: _____

21

VALIANT QUEEN ESTHER

1. Who was the Persian queen who refused to display her beauty at the court of King Ahasuerus?

2. Name Esther's cousin who adopted her.

3. What was Esther's big secret as she competed with other women to become the new queen?

4. How did King Ahasuerus declare that Esther was chosen as the new queen?

5. Who told Esther of a plot to assassinate King Ahasuerus?

6. Why did Mordecai refuse to bow to Prime Minister Haman as other citizens were doing?

7. How did Haman plan to retaliate for Mordecai's failure to bow to him?

8. How did Mordecai conduct himself after learning of the decree to kill all the Jews?

9. Who was hanged on the gallows prepared for Mordecai after Esther told the king about the plot to kill the Jews?

10. What Jewish festival commemorates a hanging and preservation of the Jews?

SCORE: _____

22

ISAIAH, GOD'S INSPIRED SEER

1. COMPLETE: Isaiah was the son of _____ and lived in _____.

2. Isaiah compared the wickedness of Jerusalem to that of what two cities destroyed during Abraham's time?

3. With what words did Isaiah accept God's call to service the year King Uzziah died?

4. COMPLETE: Isaiah prophesied that Judah would be taken by _____, but a faithful remnant would return.

5. What message was conveyed to Egypt when God told Isaiah to go naked and barefoot?

6. Isaiah prophesied that a virgin would conceive and her Son would sit on whose throne?

7. COMPLETE: Jesus began His public ministry by identifying Himself with these words from Isaiah: "The Spirit of the Lord is upon me; because he hath anointed me to
_____."

8. COMPLETE: Isaiah foretold the conversion of the Gentiles by saying that Israel would become a _____ to the Gentiles, proclaiming God's _____ unto the end of the earth.

9. COMPLETE: In Isaiah's vision of the suffering Servant, the Messiah would be _____ for our transgressions and _____ for our iniquities.

10. COMPLETE: Isaiah presented God's offer of mercy to rebellious nations: "Seek ye the LORD while he may _____, call ye upon him while he _____."

SCORE: _____

23

JEREMIAH, PROPHET OF THE NEW COVENANT

1. Why was Jeremiah reluctant to accept God's call to service?

2. Why was Jeremiah forbidden to marry?

3. Why did Jeremiah weep openly for his people?

4. What was the meaning of Jeremiah's prophecy: "Out of the north an evil shall break forth upon all the inhabitants of the land"?

5. What was the main thrust of Jeremiah's temple sermon?

6. What was the message of the clay jar broken by Jeremiah in Hinnom Valley (Tophet)?

7. CHOICE: How did King Jehoiakim react to Jeremiah's scroll prophesying doom on Judah?
   a. He repented.
   b. He issued a proclamation.
   c. He had the scroll thrown in the fire.

8. How did Jeremiah say the new covenant with Israel would be different from the old failed covenant?

9. Why was Jeremiah cast into a dungeon by King Zedekiah?

10. Where were Jeremiah and others taken after Gedaliah, governor of Judah, was murdered?

SCORE: _____

24

DANIEL AND
THE HEBREW CHILDREN

1. Daniel and other choice young men were taken to Babylon to serve in the royal court of what king?

2. What were the new names given to Daniel's three Hebrew friends?

3. What kind of diet did Daniel and his three friends choose rather than consuming the king's rich food and wine?

4. What happened to Daniel and his friends after Daniel interpreted Nebuchadnezzar's dream?

5. Why were Daniel's three friends thrown into the fiery furnace?

6. What did the king see in the blazing furnace that led him to release the three men and praise their God?

7. What did the handwriting on the wall tell Daniel would happen to King Belshazzar's kingdom?

8. What was Daniel's daily prayer practice during the reign of Darius?

9. How was Daniel delivered from the lion's den?

10. Who appeared to Daniel while he was confessing Israel's sins and praying for Jerusalem to be rebuilt and for the temple to be restored?

SCORE: _____

25

MORE PEERLESS PROPHETS OF GOD

1. Which prophet was directed by the Lord to take a prostitute as a wife?

2. What prophet was a herdsman whom God instructed, "Go, prophesy unto my people Israel"?

3. What prophet was transported into the valley of "dry bones" and told to preach to them?

4. Who was swallowed by a large fish and deposited on dry ground?

5. What prophet foretold the outpouring of God's Spirit at Pentecost?

6. Who predicted that the Savior would be born in Bethlehem?

7. Who was directed by the Lord to give his daughter a symbolic name meaning, "I will no more have mercy upon the house of Israel"?

8. Who prophesied Israel's collapse and captivity by Assyria?

9. Who addressed the Jewish captives in Babylon and foretold they would be restored to their homeland?

10. Who became angry when the people of Nineveh repented after he preached to them?

SCORE: _____

26

THE TEMPLE
AT JERUSALEM

1. While King David envisioned the temple, who actually had it constructed?

2. What king of Tyre was called on to provide materials and help design the temple?

3. In what room of the first temple was the ark of the covenant kept?

4. What king of Judah decreed that the temple in Jerusalem was the one place of prayer and sacrifice for all the people?

5. COMPLETE: Solomon's temple was destroyed by _____ in 587 B.C. and temple treasures were carried to Babylon.

6. What two prophets encouraged the construction of the second temple in Jerusalem?

7. The second temple, completed by returned exiles, is known by what name?

8. Which of Satan's three temptations of Christ involved a "pinnacle of the temple"?

9. COMPLETE: The infant Jesus was dedicated in the third temple and, during His ministry, drove out the _____.

10. Who predicted the destruction of the third temple, a prophecy fulfilled in A.D. 70?

SCORE: _____

27

JEWELS OF WISDOM

1. Who uttered this in a spirit of resignation after a series of personal calamities: "The LORD gave, and the LORD hath taken away; blessed be the name of the LORD"?

2. COMPLETE: "The fool hath said in his heart, There _____."

3. In what book of the Bible do we find these words: "In all thy ways acknowledge him, and he shall direct thy paths"?

4. COMPLETE: "Commit thy way unto the LORD; trust also in him; and he shall _____."

5. In what book of wisdom do we find these words: "Cast thy bread upon the waters: for thou shalt find it after many days"?

6. COMPLETE: A wise man said, "A good name is rather to be chosen than
_____."

7. COMPLETE: The psalmist declared: "I was glad when they said unto me, Let us go into the _____."

8. Why does this proverb advise us, "Boast not thyself of to morrow"?

9. COMPLETE: "Wine is a mocker, strong drink is raging: and whosoever is deceived thereby _____."

10. Who is the likely author of this wisdom: "Remember now thy Creator in the days of thy youth, while the evil days come not"?

SCORE: _____

28

BIBLE CURIOSITIES

1. What portion of Adam's anatomy did God remove to create a companion for the man?

2. Where did Peter find a coin to pay the temple tax?

3. What personal item did Ruth's kinsman present to Boaz as indication he would not redeem Ruth?

4. Who led a dance of joy wearing only a linen cloth when the ark of the covenant arrived in Jerusalem?

5. When Jesus healed the Gadarene demoniac, where did the demons go?

6. What king of Israel solved a child custody dispute by proposing that the child be cut in half?

7. What prophet was taken alive to heaven in a whirlwind?

8. What did Elisha instruct Captain Naaman to do to rid himself of leprosy?

9. What young prince was hidden in the temple by his aunt for six years to avoid the wrath of Queen Athaliah?

10. Who went to sleep while Paul was preaching and fell from a window to his death, but was revived by the apostle?

SCORE: _____

29

INFAMOUS FAILURES

1. What couple lost their home in a garden, suffered many hardships, and ultimately died because of their sin of disobedience?

2. Who was the judge of Israel who sacrificed his only child as an offering to God because of a rash promise made in battle with the Ammonites?

3. Which king failed to give glory to God and was struck dead by an angel and eaten by worms?

4. What enemy of Israel stole the sacred ark of the covenant and was cursed with many calamities for seven months?

5. Who was the godly judge whose sons succeeded him as judge and were so corrupt that the people demanded a king instead?

6. What king of Israel served the Lord faithfully for many years, but ultimately rejected the Lord to serve idols?

7. Who was the wealthy evil man from Carmel who refused food to David's men and was smitten by the Lord?

8. Who was the couple in the early church who died after lying about property sold and the money given to the church?

9. Who was the exorcist whose seven sons tried to duplicate the healings of Paul and were run out of the city naked and wounded by an evil spirit?

10. What did Judas say to the Jewish leaders when he tried to return the thirty pieces of silver given him to betray Jesus?

SCORE: _____

30

PALTRY EXCUSES

1. What excuse did Adam offer for eating the forbidden fruit in the Garden of Eden?

2. What excuse did Eve use for eating the forbidden fruit in the garden?

3. What was Aaron's excuse for shaping a golden calf out of women's earrings?

4. Why did Laban say he refused to give his daughter Rachel to Jacob after Jacob had worked seven years to fulfill their agreement?

5. Most of the spies who investigated Canaan said the land could not be taken for what reason?

6. After Jesus healed a man blind from birth, why did the man's parents fail to confirm the healing?

7. How did Jesus answer the reluctant disciple who said he must first bury his father before following the Master?

8. In Jesus' parable of the great feast, what excuses were made by businessmen who could not attend?

9. What excuse for not attending the great feast was offered by a man with a new companion?

10. Why did the young ruler who asked Jesus about eternal life go away "sorrowful"?

SCORE: _____

31

PAINFUL PUNISHMENTS

1. What was Adam's punishment for disobeying God in the Garden of Eden?

2. Who responded, "My punishment is greater than I can bear" when the Lord told him he was "cursed from the earth" for killing his brother?

3. Which two sons of Jacob slew all the males of Shechem's city in retaliation for a prince of the city who raped their sister Dinah?

4. Whose wife was turned into a pillar of salt for looking back at the destruction of a wicked city?

5. Who was swallowed up by the earth, along with his fellow conspirators, in a rebellion against Moses and Aaron?

6. Whose sons were consumed by fire for offering an unholy sacrifice in the tabernacle?

7. Who was denied entrance into the Promised Land for an act of impatience and faithlessness at Meribah?

8. What was Achan's sin that resulted in his being stoned to death?

9. COMPLETE: Uzzah died after accidentally touching the _____ as it was being transported to Jerusalem.

10. According to Mosaic Law, what was the punishment for one who blasphemed God's name?

SCORE: _____

32

PRAYERS THAT PREVAILED

1. COMPLETE: According to James, the effective prayers of a _____ man "availeth much."

2. Who was the godly son born to Hannah and Elkanah in answer to prayer?

3. What did Solomon request of the Lord as he began his reign?

4. Whom did Elijah defeat on Mt. Carmel when fire from heaven fell?

5. Who cried to the Lord in the wilderness when there was no water fit to drink?

6. Name the elderly priest whose wife bore a son who was a kinsman of Jesus.

7. COMPLETE: After praying to the Father, Jesus raised Lazarus from the dead with the command: "Lazarus, _____."

8. What historic outpouring of God's Spirit in Jerusalem followed an upper room prayer meeting?

9. COMPLETE: As Jesus was dying on the cross, He prayed for His enemies: "Father, forgive them; for _____

_____."

10. In Jesus' parable of two men at prayer, who prayed, "God be merciful to me a sinner"?

SCORE: _____

33

OBSERVING THE SABBATH

1. Why did God bless and sanctify the seventh day?

2. What provision did God make for the Israelites in the wilderness to have manna on the Sabbath?

3. COMPLETE: God spoke from Mt. Sinai: "Remember the sabbath day, to _____."

4. What punishment was given to a man in the wilderness for picking up sticks on the Sabbath?

5. According to Mark, what did Jesus often do in Nazareth on the Sabbath?

6. COMPLETE: After His disciples plucked corn on the Sabbath, Jesus declared: "The sabbath was made for man, and not man for the sabbath: therefore the Son of man is _____."

7. COMPLETE: Jesus healed the sick on the Sabbath, indicating that it is _____ to do good on the _____.

8. Why did Jesus call a synagogue official a hypocrite for objecting to a crippled woman's being healed on the Sabbath?

9. After what great event did Christians begin to observe the first day of the week as their Sabbath?

10. What church worshiped on the first day of the week and brought offerings for the suffering saints in Judea?

SCORE: _____

34

GUIDANCE ON GIVING

1. COMPLETE: On Mt. Sinai, the Lord told Moses that _____ of the Israelites' produce belonged to the Lord.

2. The prophet Malachi accused the Israelites of robbing God in what fashion?

3. According to Malachi, what blessing does God promise those who are faithful in bringing tithes and offerings into God's storehouse?

4. Who said in a prayer to God that he and his people couldn't really give anything to God because they were only giving back what was already His?

5. Why did Jesus commend the poor widow's two-mite offering made in the temple?

6. Why did Paul commend the generosity of the Macedonian churches to the Corinthians?

7. COMPLETE: "Every man according as he purposeth in his heart, so let him give; not grudgingly, or of necessity: for God _____."

8. What was the sin of Ananias and Sapphira that resulted in their deaths?

9. How did Paul instruct the Corinthians to raise funds for the suffering saints at Judea?

10. COMPLETE: Commending generosity, Jesus promised His followers: "Give, and _____."

SCORE: _____

35

THE BIBLE ON THE BIBLE

1. COMPLETE: "Thy word is a lamp unto my feet, and a _____ unto my path."

2. Which companion of Paul was commended for his knowledge of the Scriptures since childhood?

3. What three words endorsing the authority of the Scriptures did Jesus use three times in resisting the temptations of Satan?

4. In describing the Christian's armor, what did Paul call the Word of God?

5. Why did Jesus urge the Jews to "search the scriptures"?

6. COMPLETE: "For the prophecy came not. . . by the will of man: but holy men of God spake as they were moved _____."

7. Seekers at what place on Paul's journeys received the Word with readiness of mind and searched the Scriptures daily?

8. COMPLETE: "All scripture is given by _____ of God, and is _____ for doctrine, for reproof, for correction, for instruction in righteousness."

9. From what Scripture was the Ethiopian official reading when Philip joined him in the chariot?

10. In what Bible verse do we find these words: "For the word of God is quick, and powerful, and sharper than any twoedged sword. . .a discerner of the thoughts and intents of the heart"?

SCORE: _____

36

ANIMALS OF THE BIBLE

1. COMPLETE: After Adam and Eve sinned, God provided clothing for them made of
_____.

2. What animal did God provide as a substitute burnt offering as Abraham prepared to offer Isaac?

3. What animal spoke to Balaam when it saw the angel of the Lord?

4. COMPLETE: The psalmist said he longed for God even as a _____ panted for water brooks.

5. CHOICE: What animal did Jesus ride for His triumphal entry into Jerusalem?
   a. A donkey   b. A warhorse   c. A camel

6. What is the strongest of beasts, according to Proverbs?

7. What animal did Samson use to hold fire-brands that destroyed the grain fields of the Philistines?

8. What animals appeared out of the woods when Elisha was taunted by children?

9. Whom was Paul referring to when he warned the Philippians to "beware of dogs"?

10. COMPLETE: Peter likened Christ's atonement to a " _____ without _____ and without spot."

SCORE: _____

37

HEROIC WOMEN

1. Who disobeyed the command of Pharaoh, king of Egypt, to save the male children of the Hebrews?

2. Who defied her husband to provide food for David's men in the wilderness?

3. What Jewish queen risked her life to intercede for her people before the Persian king?

4. Who killed the Canaanite commander, Sisera, while he slept by nailing a tent peg through his head?

5. Who was the Moabite widow who left her homeland to follow her mother-in-law to Bethlehem?

6. What woman of Jericho gave lodging and protection to Joshua's spies?

7. Who hid her young nephew, Prince Joash, in the temple for six years to avoid the wrath of Queen Athaliah?

8. Where did the widow live who fed the prophet Elijah from her last handful of meal?

9. What friend of Jesus braved the early morning darkness alone to visit His tomb?

10. Who was the businesswoman from Thyatira who opened her home to Paul and the saints after her conversion?

SCORE: _____

38

A SAVIOR IS BORN

1. Who was the Roman emperor who ordered the census requiring Mary and Joseph to travel to Bethlehem?

2. What prophet foretold that the Messiah would be born to a virgin?

3. Name the prophet who declared the Savior would be born in Bethlehem.

4. Why was it necessary for Jesus to be born in a stable manger?

5. Who reassured the fearful shepherds in the fields around Bethlehem?

6. What sign were the shepherds told would verify the Savior's birth?

7. COMPLETE: "For unto you is born this day in the city of David a Saviour, which is _____."

8. What phenomenon led the wise men to the Savior?

9. What three gifts did the wise men bring to the infant Jesus?

10. What is the meaning of the name "Emmanuel"?

SCORE: _____

39

FROM BETHLEHEM TO THE RIVER JORDAN

1. What sacrifice did Mary and Joseph offer when Jesus was dedicated in the temple?

2. Whom did devout Simeon meet in the temple that the Spirit promised he would see before death?

3. To avoid Herod's wrath, where did Mary and Joseph take Jesus before returning to their home?

4. What ruthless command did King Herod give when he realized the wise men had deceived him?

5. In what town of Galilee did Jesus spend His early years?

6. Where was young Jesus found when He was missing for three days after the Feast of the Passover?

7. COMPLETE: "And Jesus increased in wisdom and stature, and in favour with _____."

8. How did Jesus answer John's reluctance to baptize Him?

9. How did the Spirit of God manifest Himself at the baptism of Jesus?

10. What did the voice from heaven say after Jesus was baptized?

SCORE: _____

40

FORERUNNER FOR THE KING

1. The ministry of John the Baptist as Christ's forerunner was foretold by which prophet?

2. Who were John's godly parents?

3. COMPLETE: John's message in the wilderness of Judea: "Repent ye: for the kingdom of heaven _____."

4. Why was John reluctant to baptize Jesus?

5. COMPLETE: John bore witness: "I am not the Christ, but that I am _____."

6. Why was John cast in prison by King Herod?

7. While in prison John sent two disciples to ask Jesus a question. What was it?

8. What did the dancing daughter of Herodias request of King Herod at his birthday party?

9. COMPLETE: Jesus paid this tribute to John: "Among them that are born of women there hath not risen a _____ _____."

10. COMPLETE: John's estimate of Christ: "He must increase, but I _____."

SCORE: _____

41

JESUS' TEMPTATIONS AND OURS

1. Why was Jesus hungry when the tempter came to Him in the wilderness?

2. How did Jesus reject Satan's temptation to turn stones into bread?

3. What was Jesus' response when Satan tempted Him to jump from the pinnacle of the temple?

4. What was Christ asked to do when Satan showed Him the kingdoms of the world?

5. Who ministered to Jesus after Satan left Him?

6. What counsel did Jesus give His sleepy disciples in Gethsemane in order to avoid temptation?

7. COMPLETE: According to Paul, everyone is tempted, but God will not allow the believer to be tempted _____.

8. COMPLETE: In His model prayer, Jesus taught us to pray: "Lead us not into temptation, but _____."

9. COMPLETE: According to Peter, "The Lord knoweth how to deliver the godly _____."

10. According to James, what has the Lord promised those who endure trials and temptations?

SCORE: _____

42

BLESSED BEATITUDES

1. COMPLETE: Jesus said the kingdom of heaven belongs to the _____.

2. COMPLETE: "Blessed are they that mourn: for they _____."

3. According to the Beatitudes, who will inherit the earth?

4. COMPLETE: Those who "hunger and thirst after righteousness" shall _____.

5. COMPLETE: "Blessed are the _____: for they shall see God."

6. What group of people will be called "the children of God"?

7. Why does Christ advise those "persecuted for righteousness sake" to rejoice?

8. COMPLETE: The psalmist declared,
   "Children are an heritage of the LORD; . . .
   _____ is the man that hath his quiver full
   of them."

9. Jesus said, "If ye know these things, happy are
   ye _____."

10. COMPLETE: Peter wrote, "If ye suffer
    _____, happy are ye."

SCORE: _____

43

THE CHRISTIAN'S EXAMPLE

1. Who referred to believers as "salt of the earth"?

2. COMPLETE: "Ye are the light of the world. A city that is set on an hill _____."

3. Why did Jesus encourage believers, "Let your light so shine before men"?

4. COMPLETE: Paul charged Roman Christians not to eat meat, drink wine, or anything to cause a brother to _____.

5. COMPLETE: Peter said it is God's will that the well doing of Christians will "silence the ignorance of _____."

6. Who said, "Follow my example, as I follow the example of Christ"?

7. Who counseled believing wives to be submissive to unbelieving husbands who might be won to Christ by the wives' Christian conduct?

8. COMPLETE: Jesus said, "If any man will come after me, let him deny himself, and take up his cross, _____."

9. What young minister was admonished to be an example to believers in word, conduct, and faith?

10. COMPLETE: Paul to Timothy: "And the things that thou hast heard of me among many witnesses, the same commit thou to faithful men, who shall be able _____."

SCORE: _____

44

FULFILLING GOD'S LAW

1. What were the Ten Commandments engraved on?

2. Where did the Levite priests store the Ten Commandments in the temple?

3. COMPLETE: Israel's captivity in Assyria was due to their leaving God's commandments to
   _____.

4. Who wrote that the purpose of the law was to give knowledge of sin and establish guilt?

5. COMPLETE: Jesus said that He came not to _____ the law, but to _____.

6. COMPLETE: Jesus taught that uncontrolled _____ was incipient murder and that _____ eyes amounted to adultery.

7. Which two commands did Jesus declare to be the greatest and the substance of all God requires?

8. What did Paul teach is the "fulfilling of the law"?

9. Who said the law was our "schoolmaster to bring us unto Christ"?

10. What was Christ's "new commandment" to His disciples before He returned to heaven?

SCORE: _____

45

HOW TO TREAT ENEMIES

1. Who was the surviving member of King Saul's family whom David showed kindness to?

2. How did Joseph answer his fearful brothers who expected retaliation after their father's death?

3. What counsel did Jesus offer those who brought gifts to the altar and had possibly offended a brother?

4. COMPLETE: According to Paul, we were reconciled to God while we were His enemies by the "_____."

5. What alternative did Christ propose rather than simply loving your neighbor and hating your enemy?

6. COMPLETE: As Christ died on the cross, He prayed, "_____, _____; for they know not what they do."

7. How did Stephen pray for his enemies as he was being stoned to death?

8. Why did the apostle Paul warn believers against avenging an enemy?

9. COMPLETE: Jesus said, "If ye forgive men their trespasses, your heavenly Father will _____."

10. COMPLETE: Peter warned Christians that our adversary, the devil, prowls like a roaring lion seeking "_____."

SCORE: _____

46

HOW TO PRAY

1. COMPLETE: The psalmist said, "If I regard iniquity in my heart, the Lord _____."

2. What blessing did Christ promise believers who prayed to the Father in secret?

3. Why did Jesus discourage long prayers and "vain repetitions"?

4. COMPLETE: Jesus said, "Ask, and it shall be given you; seek and ye shall find; knock, _____."

5. How did Jesus spend the night before choosing the apostles?

6. What were Peter, James, and John doing while Jesus was praying and agonizing in Gethsemane?

7. What was Paul's "heart's desire and prayer to God" for Israel?

8. COMPLETE: Paul charged the Philippians: "Be careful for nothing; but in every thing by prayer and supplication with thanksgiving let your _____ unto God."

9. What did James advise those who were lacking in wisdom to do?

10. COMPLETE: John declared, "This is the confidence that we have in him, that, if we ask any thing _____, he heareth us."

SCORE: _____

47

PURSUING RICHES IN HEAVEN

1. COMPLETE: "A good name is rather to be chosen _____."

2. Why did Jesus say Earth's treasures are uncertain?

3. COMPLETE: Jesus said, "For where your treasure is, there will your _____."

4. COMPLETE: Jesus declared if a person had not been faithful with the "unrighteous mammon, who will commit to your trust the _____?"

5. What did Jesus require of the wealthy young ruler who desired eternal life?

6. In Jesus' parable of the rich farmer, why did He call the man a "fool"?

7. Whom did Paul instruct to counsel the "rich in this world" to trust in the living God rather than their "uncertain riches"?

8. COMPLETE: Paul's testimony: "My God shall supply all your need according to his _____."

9. In Jesus' parable of the pearl of great price, what did the merchant do when he discovered a pearl of tremendous value?

10. COMPLETE: "Seek ye first the kingdom of God, and his righteousness; and _____ shall be added unto you."

SCORE: _____

48

JESUS AND
HIS APOSTLES

1. Who was the first apostle chosen by Jesus?

2. What three apostles are regarded as members of Christ's inner circle?

3. What apostle was a disciple of John the Baptist when Jesus enlisted him?

4. Who was the tax collector chosen as an apostle?

5. Who were the two sons of Zebedee chosen as apostles?

6. To which apostle did Christ commit the "keys of the kingdom"?

7. Which apostle did Jesus describe as an Israelite without guile?

8. What was purchased with the thirty pieces of silver Judas threw on the temple floor?

9. Who replaced Judas as an apostle?

10. While dying on the cross, Christ committed the care of His mother to which apostle?

SCORE: _____

49

JESUS AND
SPECIAL FRIENDS

1. Whom did Jesus dine with after the Lord raised him from the dead?

2. What believing friend of Jesus prepared the Savior's body for burial and placed Him in his own tomb?

3. What man helped Jesus carry His cross?

4. Who had a dialogue with Jesus about the new birth and helped prepare Christ's body for burial?

5. Which friend did Jesus first meet in a tree near Jericho?

6. What unnamed woman from Samaria did Jesus offer the "living water" to?

7. What friend did Jesus deliver from "seven devils"?

8. Who anointed Jesus' feet at her home in Bethany?

9. Who grieved at the death of her brother and appealed to Jesus for help?

10. Whose mother asked Jesus to give her sons places of honor in His coming kingdom?

SCORE: _____

50

JESUS AND
THE CHILDREN

1. COMPLETE: Calling a child to join Him, Jesus told His hearers, "Except ye be converted and become _____, ye shall not enter. . .heaven."

2. CHOICE: Jesus said that anyone offending "one of these little ones which believe in me" would suffer a fate worse than which of the following?
   a. Stoning
   b. Embarrassment
   c. Drowning

3. In what town of Galilee was Jesus when He healed a nobleman's son who was near death in Capernaum?

4. What was the disciples' reaction to those who brought little children to Jesus to be blessed?

5. How did mourners respond when Jesus told them that Jairus's daughter was only sleeping?

6. After Jesus cleansed the temple in Jerusalem, what perceptive praise came from children?

7. COMPLETE: Jesus said that if imperfect fathers gave good gifts to their children, "how much more shall your heavenly Father give the _____ to them that ask him?"

8. COMPLETE: Jesus compared the unbelieving "men of this generation" to whining children playing games in the _____.

9. Affectionately calling His disciples "little children," Jesus gave a new commandment. What was it?

10. COMPLETE: According to Jesus, the person who humbles himself as a child is _____ in the kingdom of heaven.

SCORE: _____

51

WOMEN WHO FOLLOWED JESUS

1. Name two of the three Marys who stood by the cross of Jesus.

2. How much did the poor widow whom Jesus commended put in the temple treasury?

3. Why did Jesus defend Mary's extravagant use of ointment when she anointed Him at Bethany?

4. COMPLETE: Jesus said to the woman caught in the act of adultery: "Neither do I condemn thee: _____."

5. How did the woman with an issue of blood express her faith in Jesus?

6. Who was the elderly prophetess who rejoiced at seeing young Jesus at His presentation in the temple?

7. COMPLETE: Joanna and Susanna, along with Mary Magdalene, were among the women who supported Jesus _____ _____.

8. Whose mother-in-law was healed of a high fever by Jesus and arose to serve her guests?

9. After Jesus told a Syrophenician woman with a sick daughter that the children's food should not be given to dogs, what was her response that pleased Jesus?

10. What did Jesus offer the Samaritan woman at the well in Sychar?

SCORE: _____

52

JESUS, THE MIRACLE WORKER

1. Jesus' first recorded miracle was at Cana of Galilee. What was it?

2. How did the disciples react when Jesus calmed the angry winds and water on the Sea of Galilee?

3. Whom did Jesus heal in Capernaum, from a distance?

4. Why was the lame man Jesus healed by the sheep market pool criticized by the Jews?

5. How did Simon Peter respond when a great amount of fish was caught after following Jesus' instructions?

6. When ten lepers approached Jesus for healing, what instructions did He give them?

7. What did Jesus say when He healed the woman who had suffered with a crooked back for eighteen years?

8. What did Jesus say to Jairus, the synagogue ruler, when Jesus was told the ruler's daughter had died?

9. How did the disciples react when they saw Jesus walking on the waters of Galilee in the storm?

10. What did blind Bartimaeus cry out to Jesus when he heard that Jesus was near Jericho?

SCORE: _____

53

FEEDING THE MULTITUDES

1. What did the disciples recommend to Jesus when He was ministering to a hungry multitude in a desert place?

2. How did Jesus respond to the disciples' recommendation for feeding the hungry people in the desert?

3. How much food did the disciples find among the crowd in the desert?

4. What did Jesus do before breaking the bread and giving it to the disciples for distribution?

5. How many baskets of food were gathered after all the people were fed?

6. How many men were fed in the desert besides the women and children?

7. After ministering for three days at a mountain in Galilee, what did Jesus tell His disciples about the hungry people?

8. After seven loaves and a few fish were discovered in the crowd, what did Jesus command the people to do?

9. How many men were fed on the mountain in addition to the women and children?

10. COMPLETE: Jesus said, "I am the bread of life: he that cometh to me _____."

SCORE: _____

54

THE DIVINE SHEPHERD

1. COMPLETE: "The LORD is my shepherd; I shall _____."

2. Why did the psalmist say he would "fear no evil" in spite of walking in the "shadow of death"?

3. COMPLETE: "Thou preparest a table before me in the _____."

4. What did the psalmist say would follow him "all the days of my life"?

5. The Shepherd Psalm ends with what comforting assurance for the future of all believers?

6. Who said, "I am the good shepherd: the good shepherd giveth his life for the sheep"?

7. How did Jesus describe one who enters the sheepfold other than by the door?

8. "But he that entereth in by the door is the
_____."

9. COMPLETE: Jesus said, "My sheep hear my voice, and I know them, and
_____."

10. Who wrote, "And when the chief Shepherd shall appear, ye shall receive a crown of glory that fadeth not away"?

SCORE: _____

55

FAILING THE FRUIT TEST

1. COMPLETE: Jesus said, "Enter ye in at the strait gate: for wide is the gate, and broad is the way, that _____."

2. COMPLETE: Jesus warned against false prophets who come in sheep's clothing, "but inwardly they are _____."

3. How did Jesus tell us to distinguish between a good tree and a corrupt tree?

4. What did Jesus say was the fate of the corrupt tree?

5. COMPLETE: Jesus said, "Not every one that saith unto me, Lord, Lord, shall enter into the kingdom of heaven; but he that doeth _____."

6. How will Jesus dismiss the hypocrites and false prophets in the final judgment?

7. What kind of believer did Jesus liken to a man who built his house upon a rock?

8. COMPLETE: Jesus said, "A good man out of the good treasure of the heart bringeth forth _____."

9. What happened when Jesus condemned an unproductive fig tree?

10. How did Paul counsel the Ephesians to deal with the "unfruitful works of darkness"?

SCORE: _____

56

MARRIAGE
AND DIVORCE

1. Who was responsible for the first wedding recorded in the Bible?

2. What privileges did the Mosaic Law give a man during his first year of marriage?

3. COMPLETE: Jesus enjoined permanence in marriage with this command: "What therefore God hath joined together, let not _____."

4. Where did Jesus attend a wedding at which the wine was exhausted?

5. COMPLETE: Paul counseled: "Husbands, love your wives, even as Christ also loved the church, and _____."

6. Peter advised believing wives to submit themselves to unbelieving husbands for what high purpose?

7. Why did Jesus say Moses permitted men to issue a bill of divorcement?

8. According to Matthew's account, what did Jesus say is the one permissible reason for divorce?

9. In what New Testament book is this statement: "Marriage is honorable among all, and the bed undefiled; but fornicators and adulterers God will judge"?

10. COMPLETE: "Let every one of you in particular so love his wife even as himself"; and the wife should _____.

SCORE: _____

57

GREATNESS IN THE KINGDOM

1. According to Matthew's account, who accompanied James and John to request high places for them in Christ's coming kingdom?

2. How did Jesus respond to the request of James and John's mother for those places of honor in His kingdom?

3. Who did Jesus say would award places of honor in the coming kingdom?

4. CHOICE: Which word describes the attitude of the other apostles to this request of James and John?
   a. Approving   b. Indifferent   c. Indignant

5. COMPLETE: Jesus said that anyone who wanted to be great should be _____.

6. COMPLETE: Jesus said He came not to be
   ministered to, but to minister and give His life
   a " _____."

7. In describing a guest of honor and a servant at
   a banquet, which did Jesus identify with?

8. In His discussion of the commandments, who
   did Jesus say would be called "great" in the
   kingdom of heaven?

9. How did Peter react when Jesus prepared to
   wash his feet prior to the Passover?

10. What did Jesus command the disciples to do
    after He had washed their feet?

SCORE: _____

58

POINTS FROM PARABLES

1. Why did Jesus say He taught in parables?

2. In Jesus' parable of the sower, what does the seed represent?

3. In the parable of the lost sheep, what did the owner of the sheep say to his neighbors when the sheep was found?

4. In the parable of the treasure hidden in a field, what did the man do in order to possess the treasure?

5. In the parable of the new wine, why did Jesus say new wine should not be put in old wineskins?

6. In the parable, what kind of disciple did Jesus indicate built his house upon a rock?

7. In the parable of the laborers in the vineyard, why did the workmen hired early in the day complain when they were paid?

8. In the parable of the pounds, why was the servant who was given only one pound to invest required to give his pound to the man who had ten?

9. In the parable of the final judgment, how did the Lord answer the righteous who asked when they had fed him or given him a drink?

10. In the parable of the rich man and Lazarus, where did the poor beggar go when he died?

SCORE: _____

59

THE PRODIGAL AND HIS FAMILY

1. COMPLETE: Jesus related the parable of the prodigal to answer the _____ and _____ who accused Him of eating with sinners.

2. How had the younger son wasted his inheritance, according to the parable?

3. What job did the prodigal take in his desperation?

4. What did the prodigal resolve to do when he "came to himself"?

5. CHOICE: What was the father's mood when he saw his prodigal son returning?
   a. Angry
   b. Compassionate
   c. Indifferent

6. What were the prodigal's first words to his father upon his return?

7. What gifts did the father bestow upon his returning son?

8. CHOICE: What was the elder brother's attitude toward his returning prodigal brother?
   a. Angry
   b. Compassionate
   c. Indifferent

9. With what words did the father reassure his elder son?

10. What reason did the father give for the lavish celebration?

SCORE: _____

60

THE SAMARITAN AND THE WOUNDED TRAVELER

1. COMPLETE: The occasion for the parable of the good Samaritan was a lawyer who asked Jesus, "What shall I do to _____?"

2. What question did the lawyer ask Jesus after He told him to love God supremely and love his neighbor as himself?

3. What condition was the traveler in when the thieves left him?

4. Who was first to observe the wounded man?

5. What did the Levite do when he saw the wounded traveler?

6. CHOICE: What was the Samaritan's attitude when he saw the wounded victim?
   a. Revulsion   b. Indifference   c. Compassion

7. What kind of first aid was the wounded victim given on the road?

8. Where was the wounded traveler taken by the man who rescued him?

9. What did the Samaritan say to his host when he left the next day?

10. After the lawyer agreed that the person showing mercy was the true neighbor, what did Jesus instruct him to do?

SCORE: _____

61

NICODEMUS MEETS JESUS

1. What were Nicodemus's credentials as a Jewish leader?

2. What compliment did Nicodemus pay Jesus when they met?

3. COMPLETE: Jesus told Nicodemus: "Except a man be born again, he cannot see _____."

4. How did Nicodemus react to Jesus' statement that a man must have a second birth?

5. What did Jesus compare the sovereignty of the Spirit to?

6. COMPLETE: "As Moses lifted up the serpent in the wilderness, even so must the _____ be lifted up."

7. COMPLETE: "For God sent not his Son into the world to condemn the world; but that the world through him _____."

8. How did Jesus express unbelieving man's condemnation in terms of darkness and light?

9. How did Nicodemus defend Jesus when the Jewish leaders were trying to apprehend Him?

10. How did Nicodemus express devotion to Jesus after He was crucified?

SCORE: _____

62

ZACCHAEUS FINDS JESUS

1. What high office did Zacchaeus hold when Jesus met him?

2. Why did Zacchaeus expect to have difficulty seeing Jesus?

3. COMPLETE: Jesus said: "Zacchaeus, make haste, and come down; for to day I must _____."

4. Jesus met Zacchaeus on the outskirts of what city?

5. How did Zacchaeus respond to Jesus' command to come down from the tree?

6. How did the crowd react to Jesus' friendship with Zacchaeus?

7. What did Zacchaeus volunteer to do for the poor after his encounter with Jesus?

8. How did Zacchaeus pledge to rectify anything he had taken by "false accusation"?

9. How did Jesus declare that Zacchaeus had become a saved man?

10. COMPLETE: Jesus said, "For the Son of man is come to seek and save _____."

SCORE: _____

63

JESUS AND THE WOMAN AT THE WELL

1. What was Jesus' destination when He left Judea and passed through Samaria?

2. In what city of Samaria did Jesus meet the woman at Jacob's well?

3. What did Jesus request from the Samaritan woman He met at the well?

4. Why was the woman at the well surprised when Jesus spoke to her?

5. COMPLETE: Jesus told the woman: "Whosoever drinketh of the water that I shall give him _____."

6. How many husbands had the Samaritan woman been married to?

7. Where did the Samaritan woman say her ancestors worshiped rather than in Jerusalem?

8. COMPLETE: "True worshippers shall worship the Father in spirit and in truth: for the Father seeketh _____."

9. What did the Samaritan woman tell the men of the city about Jesus?

10. How did numerous people of the city respond to the testimony of the Samaritan woman?

SCORE: _____

64

FROM PALM SUNDAY TO CALVARY

1. As Jesus rode into Jerusalem on Palm Sunday, what was His reaction as He looked over the city?

2. COMPLETE: Jesus cleansed the temple a second time with this charge: "My house shall be called. . .the house of prayer. . .but ye have made it a _____."

3. When Jewish leaders challenged Jesus' authority to cleanse the temple, what question did Jesus ask in response?

4. COMPLETE: Paul said, "For as often as ye eat this bread, and drink this cup, ye do shew _____."

5. What did Jesus advise the disciples to do when He first found them asleep in the Garden of Gethsemane?

6. How did the Jewish leaders know where to find Jesus in the Garden of Gethsemane?

7. What did Peter do in defense of Jesus after His accusers arrived in the garden?

8. What charge was made by false witnesses against Jesus, before Caiaphas, the high priest?

9. What did Pilate say to the crowd when he questioned Jesus the second time and washed his hands?

10. How did the soldiers mock Jesus as a king when they took Him to be crucified?

SCORE: _____

65

ANATOMY OF A TRAITOR

1. Whose name always comes last in the Gospels' lists of the twelve apostles?

2. What office did Judas occupy among the apostles?

3. COMPLETE: "Judas, the brother of James, and Judas Iscariot, which also _____."

4. What was Judas's criticism of Mary when she anointed Jesus at Bethany?

5. Whom did Judas contact about betraying Jesus?

6. How much money was Judas promised for betraying Jesus?

7. After Jesus identified Judas as the betrayer at the Last Supper, what did Jesus say to Judas?

8. How did Judas identify Jesus in the Garden of Gethsemane?

9. What did Judas do after throwing the silver on the temple floor?

10. COMPLETE: Jesus said, "Woe unto that man by whom the Son of man is betrayed! it had been good for that man if he _____."

SCORE: _____

66

FROM TRAGEDY TO TRIUMPH

1. What was Jesus offered to drink as He approached Golgotha?

2. What did the sign say that was posted above Jesus' head on the cross?

3. What request did the repentant thief on the cross next to Jesus make of the Savior?

4. What words did Jesus use when He committed His mother to John's care?

5. What happened to the sky between the sixth and ninth hours as Jesus approached death?

6. What were Jesus' final words before His death?

7. As Jesus died, what phenomenon happened in the temple?

8. Which two friends of Jesus prepared His body for burial?

9. Who rolled away the stone from the entrance to Jesus' tomb?

10. How did Mary Magdalene announce to the disciples that Jesus had risen from the dead?

SCORE: _____

67

CHRIST'S
RESURRECTION AND OURS

1. What did Jesus invite "doubting Thomas" to do that would affirm His resurrection?

2. According to the apostle Paul, how many people saw the risen Christ at one time?

3. COMPLETE: Jesus said it was the Father's will that those who trusted Him would have eternal life and _____ at the last day.

4. To which church did Paul offer this testimony: "Knowing that he which raised up the Lord Jesus shall raise up us also by Jesus, and shall present us with you"?

5. COMPLETE: From 1 Corinthians: "And if Christ be not risen, then is our preaching vain, and _____ is also vain."

6. COMPLETE: "But now is Christ risen from the dead, and become _____ of them that slept."

7. What did Paul say was the last enemy of believers to be destroyed?

8. COMPLETE: "Behold, I shew you a mystery; We shall not sleep, but we shall all _____."

9. What did Paul say is the "sting of death"?

10. What group of believers did Paul say would be the first resurrected?

SCORE: _____

68

JESUS' ASCENSION AND INTERCESSION

1. Before Christ's ascension, in what territory did He say disciples would be witnesses for Him by the Spirit's power?

2. How many days after the resurrection did Jesus ascend into heaven?

3. As Jesus ascended into heaven, who told the disciples He would return in like manner?

4. Where did the ascension of Jesus take place?

5. CHOICE: How did the disciples react after witnessing Jesus' ascension?
   a. Fearful   b. Indifferent   c. Joyous

6. What did Jesus do with His hands just prior to His ascension?

7. Whom did Jesus intercede for while He was on the cross?

8. COMPLETE: In Jesus' intercessory prayer for His disciples, He prayed: "Not that thou shouldest take them out of the world, but that thou shouldest keep them from _____."

9. COMPLETE: Christ is the believers' high priest who "ever liveth to _____ for them."

10. In what book do we find these words: "Seeing then that we have a great high priest, that is passed into the heavens, Jesus the Son of God, let us hold fast our profession"?

SCORE: _____

69

WHEN THE POWER FELL AT PENTECOST

1. COMPLETE: The prophet Joel foretold the outpouring of God's Spirit: "I will pour out my spirit _____."

2. Prior to His ascension, Jesus gave believers what instructions concerning the promised "power from on high"?

3. COMPLETE: Jesus promised the disciples that the Spirit's power would enable them to witness in Jerusalem, Judea, Samaria, and "unto the _____."

4. What was the first supernatural sign the disciples experienced at Pentecost?

5. When the "cloven tongues of fire" settled on believers, what was their reaction?

6. What language phenomenon happened to people from many nations gathered at Pentecost?

7. How did the skeptics seek to explain what was happening to believers at Pentecost?

8. COMPLETE: In his message, Peter boldly declared: "Let all the house of Israel know assuredly, that God hath made that same Jesus. . .both _____."

9. Those convicted of sin cried out, "What shall we do?" What was Peter's answer?

10. Those who believed, were baptized, and joined the fellowship after Peter's message totaled how many?

SCORE: _____

70

WITNESSES SCATTERED ABROAD

1. Where did the apostles go after an angel delivered them from a Jerusalem prison?

2. COMPLETE: When the Jewish officials reprimanded the apostles for their witness, Peter's classic response was, "We ought to obey _____."

3. Who was the respected Pharisee who told the Jewish council that if the apostles' witness "be of God, ye cannot overthrow it"?

4. Which of the seven "deacons" was described as "full of faith and power" and one who "did great wonders and miracles among the people"?

5. What were the false charges that led to Stephen's death by stoning?

6. What were Stephen's last words before he died as a Christian martyr?

7. COMPLETE: "They that were scattered abroad went every where _____."

8. Which of the seven "deacons" went to the city of Samaria and "preached Christ unto them"?

9. Why did Philip leave his great work in Samaria to travel the road from Jerusalem to Gaza?

10. After the Ethiopian eunuch accepted Jesus, what did he request of Philip?

SCORE: _____

71

SIMON PETER: A PEBBLE WHO BECAME A ROCK

1. Who brought Simon Peter to Jesus?

2. COMPLETE: Peter's confession: "Thou art the Christ, the Son of _____."

3. When Jesus warned Peter that Satan desired to test him, what was Peter instructed to do after he recovered?

4. What did Peter do after his third denial of Christ and the crowing of the rooster?

5. After the Resurrection, Christ dined with the disciples on the Galilee shore and asked Peter a crucial question. What was it?

6. In his message at Pentecost, Peter quoted which prophet to convince the skeptics the disciples were not drunk?

7. What was Peter's response when a lame man asked Peter and John for money at the temple door?

8. Who was the woman disciple at Joppa whom Peter raised from the dead?

9. Where did Peter go to join other believers when he was delivered from Herod's prison?

10. What name did Jesus give Peter that was prophetic of his maturity as a Christian leader?

SCORE: _____

72

SAUL: FROM PERSECUTOR TO APOSTLE

1. Saul of Tarsus consented to the death of which Christian martyr?

2. Where was Saul headed when he left Jerusalem to persecute the Lord's people?

3. What did Saul do when a light from heaven flashed around him?

4. What did the voice from heaven say to Saul?

5. How did the Lord answer Saul's question, "What wilt thou have me to do?"

6. What physical handicap did Saul experience for three days?

7. Who was the disciple in Damascus whom the Lord directed to find and assist Saul?

8. What did the Lord say to the reluctant disciple in Damascus to convince him to help Saul?

9. After Saul was baptized and spent time with other disciples, where did he go to witness for Christ?

10. How did the Jews react to Saul's bold witness for Christ?

SCORE: _____

73

PAUL'S MISSIONARY JOURNEYS

1. How did the believers react to Paul when he returned to Jerusalem after his conversion?

2. COMPLETE: "And the disciples were called Christians first in _____."

3. How did the church at Antioch set Barnabas and Paul apart for missionary service?

4. Who was the sorcerer at Paphos who was struck blind by Paul for his heresy?

5. At Lystra, what motivated the crowd to proclaim Paul and Barnabas as gods?

6. In Paul's vision at Troas, what appeal did the man from Macedonia make?

7. When an earthquake rocked the prison at Philippi, what did the jailer cry out to Paul and Silas?

8. Why did Paul and Timothy decide not to minister in Asia and Bithynia?

9. What was Paul accused of saying in Ephesus that offended Demetrius, the silversmith?

10. COMPLETE: While praying in the temple, Paul had a vision in which the Lord said, "Depart: for I will send thee far hence _____."

SCORE: _____

74

PAUL'S
MISSIONARY COMPANIONS

1. Who interceded for Paul when the believers at Jerusalem were reluctant to accept him as a convert?

2. What missionary associate did Paul and Barnabas have a disagreement over?

3. Which missionary companion had a godly Jewish mother and a Greek father?

4. Who was Paul's companion in the jail at Philippi?

5. Name the tentmaking couple who offered hospitality to Paul in Corinth.

6. Who was the companion who chronicled much of Paul's missionary activities in Acts?

7. Which companion is described: "A certain Jew. . .born at Alexandria, an eloquent man, and mighty in the scriptures"?

8. Who brought gifts from the Philippians to Paul while he was imprisoned in Rome?

9. When Paul was near death in prison, whom did he urge to "come before winter"?

10. What traveling companion was sent by Paul to correct problems in the church at Corinth?

SCORE: _____

75

THE NAME ABOVE ALL NAMES

1. COMPLETE: From Philippians: "Wherefore God also hath highly exalted him, and given him a name which is above _____."

2. What title for the Messiah, from Isaiah, fore-tells Christ's role as a Peacemaker?

3. What was Jesus' favorite title for Himself that emphasized His humanity?

4. In what New Testament book do we find this title for Christ: "author and finisher of our faith"?

5. What title was used by the voice from heaven to describe Jesus following His baptism?

6. What phrase did Jesus use to describe Himself after feeding the five thousand men?

7. How did Jesus describe Himself after this statement: "I must work the works of him that sent me, while it is day: the night cometh, when no man can work"?

8. CHOICE: What expression did Paul use to describe Christ's sacrifice for us?
   a. Sacrificial lamb
   b. Our passover
   c. Burnt offering

9. How did Christ describe Himself to Martha prior to raising Lazarus from the dead?

10. COMPLETE: From Revelation: "I am Alpha and Omega, the _____."

SCORE: _____

76

PAUL'S VIEWS ON JOY AND SUFFERING

1. COMPLETE: "Rejoice with them that do
   _____, and weep with them that
   _____."

2. What was Paul's testimony when the prophet
   Agabus foretold that Paul would be bound up
   in Jerusalem?

3. COMPLETE: "For to you it has been granted
   on behalf of Christ, not only to believe in
   Him, but also to _____."

4. For what purpose did Paul say he had been
   given a "thorn in the flesh"?

5. COMPLETE: "Be anxious for nothing, but
   in everything by prayer and supplication, with
   thanksgiving, let your requests be
   _____."

6. To whom did Paul write: "I remember you in my prayers night and day, greatly desiring to see you, being mindful of your tears, that I may be filled with joy"?

7. According to Second Corinthians, for what high purpose does God comfort believers?

8. To which church did Paul address these words: "I now rejoice in my sufferings for you, and fill up in my flesh what is lacking in the afflictions of Christ"?

9. What did Paul tell the Corinthians that the believer's temporary "light affliction" would result in?

10. COMPLETE: "If we suffer, we shall also _____."

SCORE: _____

77

CHRIST AND HIS CHURCH

1. In establishing His church on the rock of Peter's confession, Christ made what promise to His followers?

2. Who said Christ's body was built on the foundation of the apostles and prophets and that Christ was the "chief corner stone"?

3. COMPLETE: "And he is the head of the body, the _____ . . .that in all things he might have the _____."

4. In what Bible book do we find these words: "For we are members of his body, of his flesh, and of his bones"?

5. Who wrote that church members are living stones composing a spiritual house that offers up "spiritual sacrifices, acceptable to God"?

6. COMPLETE: Paul to the Romans: "So we, being many, are one body in Christ, and every one members _____."

7. Whom was Paul addressing in this charge: "Take heed therefore unto yourselves, and to all the flock, over the which the Holy Ghost hath made you overseers, to feed the church of God"?

8. CHOICE: According to Paul, the main task of church leaders is which of the following?
   a. Erect buildings
   b. Increase offerings
   c. Perfect the saints

9. Why were the Hebrew Christians exhorted not to neglect "assembling. . .together"?

10. CHOICE: According to Paul's word to the Ephesians, what kind of church should be presented to Christ?
   a. Prosperous and active
   b. Holy and blameless
   c. Loving and caring

SCORE: _____

78

ON GUARD FOR CHRIST'S RETURN

1. Where did Christ say the "gospel of the kingdom" would be preached before the world ended?

2. COMPLETE: According to Christ, the time of the Second Coming is known only to

   _____.

3. Whom will Christ send to gather the redeemed when He returns to earth?

4. COMPLETE: Jesus said, "Watch therefore: for ye know not what hour

   _____."

5. In Jesus' parable of the ten virgins, why were five foolish women not prepared to enter the bridal party?

6. In picturing the separation of the sheep and the goats at final judgment, why did the king reject those on his left hand?

7. According to Philippians, to what will Christ change our mortal bodies when He returns?

8. On what basis did Christ say persons would be rewarded at His coming?

9. According to Paul's message in Athens, what assurance has God given us that Christ will judge the world?

10. COMPLETE: Jesus' promise to believers: "If I go and prepare a place for you, I will come again, and _____"

SCORE: _____

79

COUNSEL FOR
YOUNG MINISTERS

1. To whom did Paul address these words: "Endure hardness, as a good soldier of Jesus Christ"?

2. Which young minister did Paul assign to work on the island of Crete?

3. COMPLETE: "Study to shew thyself approved unto God, a workman that needeth not to be ashamed, rightly dividing _____."

4. Why was Timothy charged to preach the word with urgency and conviction in all seasons?

5. COMPLETE: Paul to Timothy: "But watch thou in all things, endure afflictions, do the work of an _____, make full proof of thy _____."

6. COMPLETE: Paul to Timothy: "Yea, and all that will live godly in Christ Jesus shall suffer _____."

7. What did Paul tell Timothy was the root of all kinds of evil?

8. COMPLETE: "Charge them that are rich in this world, that they be not highminded, nor trust in uncertain riches, but in the _____."

9. To whom did Paul address these affectionate words: "Mine own son after the common faith"?

10. COMPLETE: Paul to Titus: "To the pure all things are pure, but to those who are defiled and unbelieving _____."

SCORE: _____

80

ACCEPTING GENTILES AS BROTHERS

1. Which Old Testament prophet foretold the conversion of the Gentiles in these words: "And the Gentiles shall come to thy light. . . the forces of the Gentiles shall come unto thee"?

2. Who was the devout Roman officer who was instructed in a vision to contact Simon Peter?

3. What was Peter doing when the Roman officer's men approached the tanner's house in Joppa?

4. What did a voice from heaven instruct hungry Peter to do when he "fell into a trance"?

5. What was Peter's response when he was instructed to eat meat that Jews regarded as "unclean"?

6. COMPLETE: "What God hath cleansed, that call not thou _____."

7. How did Cornelius receive Peter when they met at Caesarea?

8. What happened to astonish Peter's believing companions as Peter preached to Cornelius?

9. COMPLETE: The Jerusalem Council, as recorded in Acts 15, determined that Gentile believers did not have to be _____.

10. Who did Paul tell the Ephesians had broken down the wall separating Jew and Gentile?

SCORE: _____

81

GIFTS FROM THE HOLY SPIRIT

1. In Peter's sermon on the Day of Pentecost, what did he offer those who repented and were baptized in Christ's name?

2. COMPLETE: "The Spirit itself beareth witness with our spirit, that we are the _____."

3. To what church did Paul address these words: "And grieve not the holy Spirit of God, whereby ye are sealed unto the day of redemption"?

4. COMPLETE: Christ told His disciples: "I will not leave you comfortless: I will _____."

5. Who instructed believers to "try the spirits whether they are of God" or the "spirit of antichrist"?

6. COMPLETE: Paul wrote to the Romans: "We have different gifts, according to the _____."

7. CHOICE: According to Paul, those blessed with the gift of generosity should give with
   a. Cheerfulness.   b. Simplicity.   c. Mercy.

8. COMPLETE: Paul told the Romans those with the gift of prophecy should prophesy "according to the _____."

9. To what church did Paul send these words: "But one and the same Spirit works all these things, distributing to each one individually as He wills?"

10. According to Paul, what is the supreme gift of the Spirit to believers?

SCORE: _____

82

LOVE, THE MOST ABIDING VIRTUE

1. What did Jesus call "the first and great commandment"?

2. COMPLETE: Jesus said, "Greater love hath no man than this, that a man lay down his life _____."

3. COMPLETE: Jesus told His disciples: "This is my commandment, That ye love one another, as _____."

4. COMPLETE: "For God so loved the _____ that he gave his only begotten _____, that whosoever believeth in him should not perish, but have _____."

5. In what New Testament book do we find these words: "Owe no man any thing, but to love one another: for he that loveth another hath fulfilled the law"?

6. How did Paul express the futility of speaking "with the tongues of men and of angels" without charity?

7. COMPLETE: "And though I bestow all my goods to feed the poor, and though I give my body to be burned, and have not charity, it _____."

8. CHOICE: Name the most enduring virtue according to 1 Corinthians 13:
   a. Faith   b. Hope   c. Charity.

9. Who wrote these words: "Behold, what manner of love the Father hath bestowed upon us, that we should be called the sons of God"?

10. COMPLETE: "We love him, because he _____."

SCORE: _____

83

COMMITTED TO
GOD'S SERVICE

1. What constrained Paul to appeal to the Romans to present themselves as a "living sacrifice. . .unto God"?

2. How were the Roman Christians urged to avoid being "conformed to this world"?

3. COMPLETE: "Know ye not that ye are the temple of God, and that the Spirit of God _____?"

4. To which church did Paul address this challenge: "For ye are bought with a price: therefore glorify God in your body, and in your spirit, which are God's"?

5. COMPLETE: "For God hath not called us unto uncleanness, but _____."

6. COMPLETE: "The Spirit itself beareth witness with our spirit, that we are the _____."

7. COMPLETE: "And grieve not the holy Spirit of God, whereby ye are sealed _____."

8. What church was challenged to speak the truth in love and grow up to be Christlike in all things?

9. To which associate did Paul write these words: "Who gave himself for us, that he might redeem us from all iniquity, and purify unto himself a peculiar people, zealous of good works"?

10. COMPLETE: Paul urged the Philippians to be blameless, shining as "lights in the world" among a "_____."

SCORE: _____

84

OBLIGATION TO A WEAK BROTHER

1. What Old Testament book contains this admonition: "Strengthen the weak hands, and make firm the feeble knees. Say to those who are fearful-hearted, 'Be strong, do not fear!' "?

2. Who addressed these words to the Ephesian elders: "I have shown you in every way, by laboring like this, that you must support the weak"?

3. COMPLETE: "Let us not therefore judge one another any more: but judge this rather, that no man put a stumblingblock or an occasion to fall in _____."

4. What type of Christian does Paul urge to "bear the infirmities of the weak," and not to please themselves?

5. COMPLETE: Paul to the Corinthians: "To the weak I became as weak, that I might win the weak. I have become all things to all men, that I might by all means
_____."

6. COMPLETE: "All things are lawful for me, but all things are not expedient: all things are lawful for me, but all things _____."

7. In Paul's discussion of abuses during the Lord's Supper, to what did he attribute many who "are weak and sickly among you"?

8. In Paul's discussion of Christian liberty, what warning did he issue about eating meat offered to idols?

9. Why did Paul counsel the "spiritual" believers to restore fallen brothers in a spirit of gentleness?

10. COMPLETE: God's answer to Paul's request to have his "thorn in the flesh" removed: "My grace _____."

SCORE: _____

85

THE CHRISTIAN'S OBLIGATION AS CITIZEN

1. Where were the Hebrew captives when Jeremiah advised them to "seek the peace of the city"?

2. Why did Paul charge the Romans to be subject to "higher powers" of authority?

3. COMPLETE: Jesus said, "Render therefore unto _____ the things which are Caesar's; and unto _____ the things that are _____."

4. COMPLETE: "For he [the ruler] is God's minister to you for _____. . .for he does not bear the _____."

5. What reason other than fear did Paul give for the Christian to submit to those in authority?

6. Whom did Paul advise to pray "for kings, and for all that are in authority"?

7. Who wrote these words to believers in Asia Minor: "Honour all men. Love the brotherhood. . . . Honour the king"?

8. Why did Paul say a Christian should pay taxes to civil authorities?

9. Upon being released from prison for preaching Christ, who told the authorities: "We ought to obey God rather than men"?

10. Where did Paul tell the Philippians the Christian's ultimate citizenship is located?

SCORE: _____

86

AMBASSADORS FOR CHRIST

1. What Old Testament prophet did God assign as a "watchman unto the house of Israel" to warn them of coming judgment?

2. What did Jesus promise four fishermen if they would follow Him?

3. When Jesus said, "The harvest truly is great, but the labourers are few," what did He instruct the seventy disciples to do?

4. COMPLETE: Prior to His ascension, Jesus instructed the disciples, "Go ye into all the world, and preach the gospel _____."

5. COMPLETE: After His resurrection, Jesus said to His disciples: "As my Father hath sent me, even so _____."

6. Who delivered these words to the church at Rome: "And how shall they hear without a preacher? And how shall they preach, except they be sent?"

7. COMPLETE: "Therefore if any man be in Christ, he is a new creature: old things are passed away; behold, _____."

8. According to Paul, what ministry has God assigned to Christians since God "hath reconciled us to himself by Jesus Christ"?

9. What two apostles were brought before the Jewish council for preaching, and declared, "We cannot but speak the things which we have seen and heard"?

10. How did Paul express the appeal to the lost on Christ's behalf?

SCORE: _____

87

SALVATION BY GRACE THROUGH FAITH

1. In what Bible book are these words found:
"Therefore being justified by faith, we have
peace with God through our Lord Jesus
Christ: By whom also we have access. . .into
this grace"?

2. COMPLETE: "By grace are ye saved through
faith; and that not of yourselves: it is the
_____."

3. In Ephesians, why did Paul tell us salvation
could not be accomplished by "works"?

4. In Galatians, why did Paul say righteousness
could not be attained by "the law"?

5. To whom did Paul address these words: "Not
by works of righteousness which we have
done, but according to his mercy he saved us"?

6. COMPLETE: Jesus said, "I will have mercy, and not sacrifice: for I am not come to call the righteous, but _____."

7. To what important council gathering did Simon Peter give this testimony: "But we believe that through the grace of the Lord Jesus Christ we shall be saved, even as they"?

8. COMPLETE: "For God so loved the world, that he gave his only begotten Son, that whosoever believeth in him should not perish, but have _____."

9. COMPLETE: "Being justified freely by his grace through the redemption that is in _____."

10. Who wrote these word to the saints in Asia Minor: "Who are kept by the power of God through faith unto salvation ready to be revealed in the last time"?

SCORE: _____

88
WORKPLACE ETHICS

1. How did God evaluate His work after six days of creative labor?

2. To whom did God say: "In the sweat of thy face shalt thou eat bread"?

3. COMPLETE: The preacher of Ecclesiastes said: "Whatsoever thy hand findeth to do, do it _____."

4. COMPLETE: Jesus said, "I must work the works of him that sent me, while it is day: the night cometh, _____."

5. By what occupation did Paul support his ministry?

6. COMPLETE: Paul to the Thessalonians: "This we commanded you, that if any would not work, neither _____."

7. COMPLETE: Paul admonished servants to obey their masters, not with eyeservice, "but as the servants of Christ, doing the will of God _____."

8. To whom did Paul give this counsel: Masters, direct your servants without threatening, "knowing that your Master also is in heaven"?

9. Who gave this principle to a church in Asia Minor: "Whatsoever ye do in word or deed, do all in the name of the Lord Jesus"?

10. To what church did Paul write these words: "Therefore, my beloved brethren, be ye stedfast, unmoveable, always abounding in the work of the Lord. . .your labour is not in vain in the Lord"?

SCORE: _____

89

FAMILY VALUES FOR CHRISTIANS

1. What were God's first instructions to the first couple created?

2. What promise was incorporated in God's commandment "Honour thy father and thy mother"?

3. What is the meaning of "Corban," a practice adopted by some Jews to avoid caring for their parents?

4. What did Paul tell Timothy about those who do not provide for their own households?

5. COMPLETE: Paul counseled the Ephesians: "Let every one. . .so love his wife even as _____;" and the wife should "_____ her husband."

6. COMPLETE: "Children, obey your parents in the Lord: for _____."

7. Paul counseled fathers not to provoke "children to wrath," but to bring them up in what manner?

8. Whom did Paul commend for a genuine faith that also characterized his mother and grandmother?

9. Who did Paul tell Titus should teach the young women to love their husbands and children and to be discreet and chaste in behavior?

10. Whom did Jesus identify as His true kinsmen in the spirit?

SCORE: _____

90

ON GUARD FOR HOLY LIVING

1. COMPLETE: "For I am the LORD your God: ye shall therefore sanctify yourselves, and ye shall be holy; for _____."

2. Who spoke these words: "For whosoever will save his life shall lose it: but whosoever will lose his life for my sake, the same shall save it"?

3. COMPLETE: "Put on the whole armour of God, that ye may be able to stand against the _____."

4. According to Ephesians, what is the Christian's shield that equips him to "quench all the fiery darts of the wicked"?

5. Who expressed this confidence in the Philippians: "Being confident of this very thing, that He who has begun a good work in you will complete it until the day of Jesus Christ"?

6. To which church did Paul address this challenge: "And whatsoever ye do in word or deed, do all in the name of the Lord Jesus, giving thanks to God and the Father by him"?

7. To which church did Paul send these encouraging words: "But the Lord is faithful, who will establish you and guard you from the evil one"?

8. COMPLETE: Paul's testimony from prison: "For I know whom I have believed, and am persuaded that he is able to keep that which I have committed unto him _____."

9. COMPLETE: Paul to the Ephesians: "Put off. . .the old man". . .and "put on the new man, which after God is created in righteousness and _____."

10. To which missionary companion did Paul write: "Denying ungodliness and worldly lusts, we should live soberly, righteously, and godly, in this present world; looking for that blessed hope"?

SCORE: _____

91

THE LORDSHIP OF CHRIST

1. To which apostle did Jesus speak these words: "I am the way, the truth, and the life: no man cometh unto the Father, but by me"?

2. COMPLETE: "The earth is the LORD's, and the fulness thereof; the world, and they _____."

3. To whom did Peter address these words: "Nor is there salvation in any other, for there is no other name under heaven given among men by which we must be saved"?

4. In Philippians, what reason does Paul give for Christ's exaltation by the Father?

5. Who wrote these words: "For I am not ashamed of the gospel of Christ: for it is the power of God unto salvation to every one that believeth; to the Jew first, and also to the Greek"?

6. To what church did Paul address these words: "For in Him dwells all the fullness of the Godhead bodily; and you are complete in Him, who is the head of all principality and power"?

7. COMPLETE: "He [Christ] is the image of the invisible God, the firstborn _____."

8. To whom did Paul address this tribute to Christ's lordship: "The blessed and only Potentate, the King of kings, and Lord of lords"?

9. According to Ephesians, where did the Father seat Christ after raising Him from the dead?

10. What Bible book reports voices from heaven declaring: "The kingdoms of this world are become the kingdoms of our Lord, and of his Christ; and he shall reign for ever and ever"?

SCORE: _____

92

CHRIST'S SECOND COMING

1. Who offered this prayer for believers at Thessalonica: "I pray God your whole spirit and soul and body be preserved blameless unto the coming of our Lord Jesus Christ"?

2. How did Paul say the Lord would descend from heaven when He returns?

3. What did Paul, writing Titus, connect to the Christian's "blessed hope"?

4. Who issued this warning to Christians who felt the Lord's return was delayed: "The Lord is not slack concerning His promise. . .but is longsuffering toward us, not willing that any should perish"?

5. Who counseled Christians to wait patiently for the Lord, even as a "farmer waits for the precious fruit" and the "early and latter rain"?

6. According to First Thessalonians, whom will God bring with Him when Jesus returns?

7. What will happen to believers who are alive when Jesus appears in the clouds?

8. According to Second Thessalonians, what is the destiny of those who "do not know God" and those who "do not obey the gospel of our Lord Jesus Christ"?

9. COMPLETE: Jesus said, "Therefore be ye also ready: for in such an hour as ye think not the _____."

10. COMPLETE: Jesus in Revelation: "Behold, I come quickly; and my reward is with me, to give every man _____ shall be."

SCORE: _____

93

RELIGION FOR DAILY LIFE

1. What did James advise those lacking wisdom to do?

2. What did James say God regards as genuine religion in addition to caring for widows and orphans?

3. COMPLETE: James declared that "faith without works is _____."

4. James indicated we do not receive what we need from God for what reason?

5. Why did James say we don't receive what we ask of God?

6. What did James say the sick should do?

7. To what did James liken a tongue out of control?

8. COMPLETE: "For whosoever shall keep the whole law, and yet offend in one point, he is _____."

9. What did James say about the one who "knoweth to do good, and doeth it not"?

10. How did James describe the blessed benefit to one who "converteth the sinner from the error of his way"?

SCORE: _____

94

GUIDANCE FOR SPIRITUAL GROWTH

1. COMPLETE: Peter to immature Christians: "As newborn babes, desire the sincere milk of the word, that ye may _____."

2. In Ephesus, for what purpose were believers to speak "the truth in love"?

3. COMPLETE: Paul admitted he had not attained perfection and resolved to "press toward the mark for the prize of the _____ in Christ Jesus."

4. To what church did Paul offer this challenge: "That ye might walk worthy of the Lord unto all pleasing, being fruitful in every good work, and increasing in the knowledge of God"?

5. COMPLETE: Paul's secret for satisfaction: "Not that I speak in respect of want: for I have

learned, in whatsoever state I am, therewith
_____."

6. In what New Testament book do we find this precept: "But without faith it is impossible to please him"?

7. Who offered this prayerful encouragement to suffering Christians: "But the God of all grace, who hath called us unto his eternal glory by Christ Jesus. . .make you perfect, stablish, strengthen, settle you"?

8. COMPLETE: "But grow in grace, and in the knowledge of our Lord and Savior Jesus Christ. To him be glory both _____
_____."

9. COMPLETE: A benediction from Jude: "Now unto him that is able to keep you from falling, and to present you faultless before the presence of his glory with _____."

10. To which church did Paul issue this challenge: "That ye would walk worthy of God, who hath called you unto his kingdom and glory"?

SCORE: _____

95

CHRIST'S PRIESTHOOD AND OURS

1. Who is the one authentic mediator between God and man?

2. How are believers encouraged to approach our sympathizing High Priest in time of need?

3. According to Ephesians, how did Christ abolish the wall dividing Jew and Gentile and establish peace?

4. COMPLETE: The torn temple veil at the death of Christ signified that all believers have _____ to our High Priest.

5. According to Hebrews, how did Christ achieve our eternal redemption without animal sacrifices?

6. Where in the Old Testament do we find this conditional prophecy of Israel's priesthood: "Now therefore, if you will indeed obey My voice and keep My covenant, then you shall be a special treasure to Me above all people"?

7. In what New Testament book do we find this picture of the Christian's priesthood: "You are a chosen generation, a royal priesthood, a holy nation, His own special people"?

8. Who penned these words of praise to our great High Priest: "To Him who loved us and washed us from our sins in His own blood, and has made us kings and priests"?

9. COMPLETE: "Confess your trespasses to one another, and pray for one another, that you may _____."

10. In which New Testament epistle is this principle of our priesthood: "There is neither Jew nor Greek. . .slave nor free. . .male nor female; for you are all one in Christ Jesus"?

SCORE: _____

96

SUFFERING AS A CHRISTIAN

1. Who addressed these words to followers: "In the world ye shall have tribulation: but be of good cheer; I have overcome the world"?

2. COMPLETE: "Blessed are they which are persecuted for righteousness' sake: for theirs is the _____."

3. After the disciples were beaten and released by the Jewish Sanhedrin for witnessing, what attitude did they display?

4. COMPLETE: "But we glory in tribulations also: knowing that tribulation worketh _____."

5. How did Paul contrast "the sufferings of this present time" with the Christian's future glory?

6. How did Paul answer the question: "Who shall separate us from the love of Christ?"

7. COMPLETE: Paul to the Philippians: "For to you it has been granted on behalf of Christ, not only to believe in Him, but also to _____."

8. Who penned these words: "For it is better, if it is the will of God, to suffer for doing good than for doing evil"?

9. COMPLETE: "Yet if any man suffer as a Christian, let him not be ashamed; but let him _____."

10. To which suffering church in Asia Minor was this comforting message addressed: "Be thou faithful unto death, and I will give thee a crown of life"?

SCORE: _____

97

PRECIOUS PROMISES

1. COMPLETE: "In all thy ways acknowledge him, and he shall _____."

2. What is the promise of this proverb that instructs parents "Train up a child in the way he should go"?

3. Who issued this invitation: "Come unto me, all ye that labour and are heavy laden, and I will give you rest"?

4. COMPLETE: Jesus said, "Ask, and it shall be given you; seek, and ye shall find; knock, and it shall be _____."

5. What was the promise Jesus gave to those chosen and ordained to bring forth fruit "that remains"?

6. In what Old Testament book of wisdom do we find this promise: "Cast thy bread upon the waters: for thou shalt find it after many days"?

7. What did Paul promise the Galatians who did not become "weary in well doing"?

8. COMPLETE: The apostle Paul's conviction: "I can do all things through Christ _____."

9. In what New Testament book do we find this promise: "And the prayer of faith shall save the sick, and the Lord shall raise him up; and if he have committed sins, they shall be forgiven him"?

10. What did Peter promise those who humbled themselves "under the mighty hand of God"?

SCORE: _____

98

MARKS OF THE BELIEVER

1. How does John describe the state of those who "walk in the light as he is in the light"?

2. COMPLETE: "If we confess our sins, he is faithful and just to forgive us our sins, and to cleanse us _____."

3. How does John describe the person who claims to know Christ but does not keep His commandments?

4. How does John portray the person who says he is in the light, but hates his brother?

5. COMPLETE: "If anyone loves the world, the _____ is not in him."

6. What mark of the believers did John tell us was assurance that we have passed from death into life?

7. COMPLETE: "Every spirit that confesses that Jesus Christ _____ is of God."

8. What Christian virtue does John say is the victory that overcomes the world?

9. COMPLETE: "We love Him because He _____."

10. How did John describe the purpose of writing his epistles?

SCORE: _____

99

REVELATION TO SEVEN CHURCHES

1. On what island was John and what day of the week was it when Christ's revelation came to him?

2. In what Roman province were the seven churches located?

3. What did John see in the midst of the seven golden candlesticks?

4. What did the seven stars in the hand of the Son represent?

5. What charge did John bring against the church at Ephesus?

6. The church at Smyrna was under attack from what heretical group?

7. Which two churches were chastised for tolerating false teachers?

8. Which church had a reputation for good works but was dead in reality?

9. What church did John describe as one with an "open door" because of its faithfulness?

10. Why was the church at Laodicea in danger of being "spewed out" of Christ's mouth?

SCORE: _____

100

GLORIOUS NEW JERUSALEM

1. Who described the Christian's "lively [living] hope" this way: "To an inheritance incorruptible, and undefiled, and that fadeth not away, reserved in heaven for you"?

2. Who said if our earthly house is destroyed, "We have a building from God, a house not made with hands, eternal in the heavens"?

3. COMPLETE: "Beloved, now are we the sons of God, and it doth not yet appear what we shall be: but we know that, when he shall appear, we shall be like him; for we shall see _____."

4. Who were those seen in white robes around the throne of heaven who serve God "day and night in his temple"?

5. Why did a voice from heaven say, "Blessed are the dead which die in the Lord from henceforth"?

6. To what did John liken his first glimpse of the "holy city, new Jerusalem"?

7. COMPLETE: "Behold, the tabernacle of God is with men, and he will dwell with them. . . and _____."

8. Why did John say there would be no more death, sorrow, or pain in heaven?

9. Why did John not see a temple in heaven?

10. Name the Lamb's record of all who are saved, mentioned in Revelation.

SCORE: _____

ANSWERS

1: DAYS OF CREATION

1. "God." Genesis 1:1.
2. The Word/Son. John 1:1–3.
3. Spirit of God. Genesis 1:2.
4. Earth, Seas. Genesis 1:10.
5. Greater light/sun, lesser light/moon. Genesis 1:16.
6. Multiply/reproduce. Genesis 1:22.
7. Dominion. Genesis 1:26, 28.
8. Six, seventh. Genesis 2:2.
9. The Garden of Eden. Genesis 2:8.
10. It was not good that he should be alone. Genesis 2:18.

2: THE FIRST FAMILY

1. Gardener. Genesis 2:15.
2. She was taken out of man. Genesis 2:23.
3. c. Eve. Genesis 3:6.
4. Cherubims and a flaming sword. Genesis 3:24.
5. Farmer, shepherd. Genesis 4:2.
6. "Am I my brother's keeper?" Genesis 4:9.
7. Seth. Genesis 4:25.
8. Sevenfold vengeance. Genesis 4:15.
9. Enoch. Genesis 4:17.
10. Christ. 1 Corinthians 15:22.

3: NOAH AND HIS ARK

1. With God. Genesis 6:9.
2. Shem, Ham, Japheth. Genesis 6:10.
3. Noah and his family could enter the ark. Genesis 6:18.
4. Two, male, female. Genesis 6:19.
5. Forty. Genesis 7:12.
6. Ararat. Genesis 8:3–4.
7. An olive leaf. Genesis 8:11.
8. He built an altar to the Lord. Genesis 8:20.

9. No flood will destroy the earth again. Genesis 9:11.
10. Ham. Genesis 9:22, 25.

4: ABRAHAM, GOD'S SOJOURNER
1. Abram. Genesis 17:5.
2. Terah. Genesis 11:27.
3. Haran. Genesis 11:31.
4. "That I will shew thee." Genesis 12:1.
5. "I will make of thee a great nation, and I will bless thee." Genesis 12:2.
6. Famine was in the land. Genesis 12:10.
7. He feared being killed. Genesis 12:12.
8. The plain of Jordan. Genesis 13:11–12.
9. Sodom. Genesis 18:23–26.
10. A ram in the thicket. Genesis 22:12–13.

5: JACOB AND ESAU
1. Isaac and Rebekah. Genesis 25:21–26.
2. In tents/indoors. Genesis 25:27.
3. A bowl of pottage/bean soup. Genesis 25:31, 34.
4. Kill Jacob. Genesis 27:41.
5. Leah. Genesis 29:25–26.
6. Israel. Genesis 32:27–28.
7. b. Embraced. Genesis 33:4.
8. Joseph and Benjamin. Genesis 35:24.
9. Isaac. Genesis 35:29.
10. Edomites. Genesis 36:9.

6: JOSEPH AND HIS BROTHERS
1. Jacob and Rachel. Genesis 35:22, 24.
2. He was the son of Jacob's old age. Genesis 37:3.
3. Reuben. Genesis 37:21.
4. Egypt. Genesis 37:28.
5. They placed goat's blood on Joseph's coat. Genesis 37:31–32.
6. "Thou art his wife: how then can I do this great wickedness, and sin against God?" Genesis 39:9.

7. Seven years of famine. Genesis 41:29–30.
8. Each man's money. Genesis 42:25, 35.
9. Simeon. Genesis 42:19, 24.
10. I'm ready to die now that I've seen you. Genesis 46:30.

7: MOSES, AARON, AND MIRIAM

1. Jochebed. Numbers 26:59.
2. Pharaoh's daughter. Exodus 2:5–6.
3. Their mother. Exodus 2:7–8.
4. Because she drew him from the water. Exodus 2:10.
5. The Egyptian was abusing a Hebrew. Exodus 2:11–12.
6. Zipporah. Exodus 2:21.
7. Moses was not eloquent. Exodus 4:10, 14.
8. She rebelled against Moses' leadership. Numbers 12:1–2, 10.
9. He carved an idol/golden calf. Exodus 32:3–7.
10. The crossing of the Red Sea. Exodus 15:20–21.

8: FROM THE BURNING BUSH TO THE RED SEA

1. Herding sheep. Exodus 3:1–2.
2. He was standing on holy ground. Exodus 3:5.
3. "I AM THAT I AM." Exodus 3:14.
4. "They will not believe me. . .they will say, The LORD hath not appeared unto thee." Exodus 4:1.
5. "Who is the LORD, that I should obey his voice to let Israel go?" Exodus 5:2.
6. Waters turned to blood. Exodus 7:20–21.
7. They sprinkled a lamb's blood over the lintels and door-posts. Exodus 12:21–23.
8. There was not time for the dough to rise. Exodus 12:39.
9. A pillar of cloud led them by day and a pillar of fire by night. Exodus 13:21.
10. They were drowned. Exodus 14:27–30.

9: WILDERNESS WANDERINGS

1. Forty years. Exodus 16:35.
2. Jethro. Exodus 18:12, 17–22.

3. Manna/bread, quail/meat. Exodus 16:12–15.
4. Aaron and Hur. Exodus 17:12–13.
5. If you will obey Me, you will be My chosen people. Exodus 19:5.
6. Worship no god but Me. Exodus 20:3.
7. Twelve. Numbers 13:2.
8. Joshua and Caleb. Numbers 14:6–9.
9. They sinned by complaining against the Lord. Numbers 21:7–8.
10. Mt. Nebo/Pisgah. Deuteronomy 32:52; 34:1.

10: JOSHUA AND CALEB

1. They gave a favorable report. Numbers 14:6–8.
2. He placed his hands on Joshua. Numbers 27:23.
3. Rahab the harlot's. Joshua 2:18; 6:17, 23.
4. When the priests carried the ark of the covenant across. Joshua 3:3.
5. Israel crossed the Jordan on dry ground. Joshua 4:20–23.
6. Captain of the host of the Lord. Joshua 5:14.
7. The walls collapsed and the city fell. Joshua 6:16, 20.
8. Command the sun to stand still. Joshua 10:12–13.
9. Hebron. Joshua 14:12–13.
10. "As for me and my house, we will serve the LORD." Joshua 24:15.

11: GIDEON AND THE MIDIANITES

1. They did evil in the Lord's sight. Judges 6:1.
2. "The LORD is with thee, thou mighty man of valour." Judges 6:12.
3. The Lord. Judges 6:25–26.
4. A wet fleece on dry ground. Judges 6:37–40.
5. Otherwise, Israel might take credit for victory. Judges 7:2.
6. Those lapping water, using their hands, were chosen. Judges 7:6–7.
7. Trumpet, pitcher, and lamp. Judges 7:16.

8. He told the Israelites the Lord would rule over them. Judges 8:22–23.
9. An ephod/idol. Judges 8:26–27.
10. Seventy/threescore and ten. Judges 8:30.

12: SAMSON AND THE PHILISTINES
1. Israel sinned against God. Judges 13:1.
2. Nazarite. Judges 13:3–5.
3. By killing a lion. Judges 14:5–6.
4. He killed thirty men at Ashkelon. Judges 14:19.
5. With fiery torches tied to foxes' tails. Judges 15:4–5.
6. With the jawbone of an ass/donkey. Judges 15:14–15.
7. A spring opened up. Judges 15:19.
8. She lulled him to sleep in her lap. Judges 16:19.
9. Grinding at the prison mill. Judges 16:21.
10. He removed two middle columns of the building. Judges 16:29–30.

13: RUTH, NAOMI, AND BOAZ
1. There was famine in Bethlehem. Ruth 1:1–2.
2. The death of her husband and sons. Ruth 1:3–7.
3. Orpah. Ruth 1:14.
4. Wherever you go, I will go; your people will be my people, and your God will be my God. Ruth 1:16.
5. "The Almighty hath dealt very bitterly with me." Ruth 1:20.
6. Boaz. Ruth 2:3.
7. She lay at his feet. Ruth 3:3–4.
8. His own children would lose inheritance rights. Ruth 4:6.
9. David. Ruth 4:13, 17.
10. Jesus. Ruth 4:13, 17, 21–22; Matthew 1:1, 5–6.

14: SAMUEL, CROWNER OF KINGS
1. "I have asked him of the LORD." 1 Samuel 1:20.
2. "Be lent to the LORD." 1 Samuel 1:28.
3. His family would be punished because of their sin and Eli's failure to discipline his sons. 1 Samuel 3:12–14.

4. There was thunder from heaven. 1 Samuel 7:7, 10.
5. Lost donkeys. 1 Samuel 9:3, 6, 14.
6. He belonged to the least important family of the smallest tribe. 1 Samuel 9:21.
7. Thunder and rain in a dry season. 1 Samuel 12:17–18.
8. Seven. 1 Samuel 16:10, 13.
9. Judge Israel/settle disputes. 1 Samuel 7:16.
10. His sons. 1 Samuel 8:1.

15: SAUL, ISRAEL'S FIRST KING
1. Kish. 1 Samuel 9:1–2.
2. Samuel. 1 Samuel 9:27–10:1.
3. "Another heart"/a new nature. 1 Samuel 10:9.
4. Mizpeh. 1 Samuel 10:17–19, 24.
5. Philistines. 1 Samuel 13:11–12.
6. He spared King Agag and retained spoils. 1 Samuel 15:8–9, 17–19.
7. He sought a harpist. 1 Samuel 16:15–17.
8. Jonathan. 1 Samuel 18:1, 3.
9. Saul has killed thousands, and David tens of thousands. 1 Samuel 18:6–9.
10. Michal. 1 Samuel 18:27–28.

16: THE SHEPHERD BOY WHO BECAME KING
1. He was keeping the sheep. 1 Samuel 16:11.
2. Harpist. 1 Samuel 16:18, 23.
3. The Lord had saved him from lions and bears; He would save David from the Philistine. 1 Samuel 17:36–37.
4. Sling and stone. 1 Samuel 17:50.
5. He threw a spear at him twice. 1 Samuel 18:11.
6. He presented to Saul the foreskins of 200 dead Philistines, twice the required number. 1 Samuel 18:25–27.
7. He shot arrows beyond him. 1 Samuel 20:20–22.
8. A piece of Saul's robe. 1 Samuel 24:4–6.
9. His widow Abigail. 1 Samuel 25:40–41.
10. Hebron. 2 Samuel 2:3–4.

17: KING DAVID OF ISRAEL

1. Jerusalem. 2 Samuel 5:5–7.
2. The sound of marching in the treetops. 2 Samuel 5:24.
3. Uzzah touched the ark and died. 2 Samuel 6:6–10.
4. Last forever. 2 Samuel 7:16–17.
5. Because of David's devotion to Jonathan, Mephibosheth's father. 2 Samuel 9:1, 6–7.
6. The sword would not depart from his house and his descendants would die violently. 2 Samuel 12:10–11.
7. "I shall go to him, but he shall not return to me." 2 Samuel 12:23.
8. Absalom. 2 Samuel 13:28–29.
9. Joab killed the king's son with his spears (or darts) while Absalom was hanging from a tree. 2 Samuel 18:14–15.
10. The king arranged for Solomon to ride David's mule with court officers. 1 Kings 1:33–39.

18: KING SOLOMON'S WISDOM AND FOLLY

1. Bathsheba. 2 Samuel 12:24.
2. Adonijah. 1 Kings 2:15, 22–24.
3. Long life. 1 Kings 3:14.
4. Cut the live child in two and give each woman half. 1 Kings 3:23–25.
5. King Hiram of Tyre. 1 Kings 5:1, 5, 8.
6. He drafted forced labor from Israel. 1 Kings 5:13.
7. The queen of Sheba. 1 Kings 10:1, 6, 10.
8. They turned him away from God to worship foreign gods. 1 Kings 11:1–4.
9. Jeroboam. 1 Kings 11:38–40.
10. Proverbs, Ecclesiastes, and Song of Solomon. 1 Kings 4:32.

19: KING AHAB AND JEZEBEL

1. Samaria. 1 Kings 16:28–29.
2. Temple to Baal. 1 Kings 16:31–32.
3. "Is that you, you troubler of Israel?" 1 Kings 18:17 (NIV).
4. Obadiah. 1 Kings 18:3–4.

5. They were killed by Elijah at Kishon Brook. 1 Kings 18:40.

6. May the gods strike me dead if I don't do the same thing to you by this time tomorrow. 1 Kings 19:1–2.

7. Dogs will lick up your blood where they licked up Naboth's blood. 1 Kings 21:19.

8. He was put in prison on bread and water. 1 Kings 22:26–27.

9. Blood washed out of Ahab's chariot was licked by dogs. 1 Kings 22:37–38.

10. He had her thrown out of a palace window, where she died, and dogs ate her flesh. 2 Kings 9:31–36.

20: ELIJAH AND ELISHA

1. By the ravens. 1 Kings 17:1–4.

2. She would not lack meal or oil until rain came. 1 Kings 17:14–15.

3. Her son. 1 Kings 17:20–22.

4. You are disobeying the Lord and worshiping the idols of Baal. 1 Kings 18:18.

5. They threw themselves on the ground saying: "The LORD, He is God!" 1 Kings 18:39 (NKJV).

6. A little cloud no bigger than a man's hand. 1 Kings 18:43–44.

7. Seven thousand remain in Israel who have not followed Baal. 1 Kings 19:10, 18.

8. He cast his mantle/cloak on him. 1 Kings 19:19.

9. He told his parents farewell and killed and prepared a dinner of his oxen. 1 Kings 19:20–21.

10. A "double portion" of Elijah's spirit. 2 Kings 2:9.

21: VALIANT QUEEN ESTHER

1. Vashti. Esther 1:11–12.

2. Mordecai. Esther 2:7.

3. She was Jewish. Esther 2:10.

4. He placed the royal crown on her and gave a banquet for her. Esther 2:17–18.

5. Mordecai. Esther 2:21–22.
6. Because Mordecai was a Jew. Esther 3:2, 4.
7. He sought to destroy all Jews in the kingdom. Esther 3:5–6.
8. He tore his clothes, dressed in sackcloth, and walked the streets, wailing. Esther 4:1.
9. Haman. Esther 7:4–6, 9–10.
10. Purim. Esther 9:21–23, 26.

22: ISAIAH, GOD'S INSPIRED SEER

1. Amoz, Jerusalem. Isaiah 1:1.
2. Sodom and Gomorrah. Isaiah 1:8–13.
3. "Here am I; send me." Isaiah 6:8.
4. Assyria. Isaiah 1:2–9; 11:11.
5. Egypt would be taken by Assyria and put to shame. Isaiah 20:3–4.
6. David's. Isaiah 7:14; 9:7.
7. "Preach good tidings." Isaiah 61:1; Luke 4:18–19.
8. Light, salvation. Isaiah 49:6.
9. Wounded, bruised. Isaiah 53:5.
10. "Be found," "is near." Isaiah 55:6.

23: JEREMIAH, PROPHET OF THE NEW COVENANT

1. I don't know how to speak; I am too young. Jeremiah 1:6.
2. Perilous times were coming; children would die and remain unburied. Jeremiah 16:2–4.
3. Because of their sins and disobedience. Jeremiah 9:1–5.
4. Nebuchadnezzar would invade from Babylon. Jeremiah 1:14; 39:1.
5. "Amend your ways" and forsake idolatry. Jeremiah 7:3, 9–10.
6. God will break the city as the jar is broken without repair. Jeremiah 19:10–11.
7. c. He had the scroll thrown in the fire. Jeremiah 36:23.
8. It would be written on their hearts. Jeremiah 31:31–33.

9. He said all remaining in the city would die; those leaving for Babylon would be saved. Jeremiah 38:1–6.
10. Egypt. Jeremiah 43:5–7.

24: DANIEL AND THE HEBREW CHILDREN

1. Nebuchadnezzar. Daniel 1:1–6.
2. Shadrach, Meshach, and Abednego. Daniel 1:7.
3. Pulse/vegetables and water. Daniel 1:12.
4. All were given high positions. Daniel 2:48–49.
5. They failed to bow down to the gold statue of the king. Daniel 3:14–15.
6. He saw four men in the furnace; the fourth looked like the Son of God. Daniel 3:25.
7. It would be divided and given to the Medes and Persians. Daniel 5:28.
8. He prayed three times daily with his windows opened toward Jerusalem. Daniel 6:10.
9. An angel shut the lions' mouths. Daniel 6:22.
10. Gabriel. Daniel 9:21.

25: MORE PEERLESS PROPHETS OF GOD

1. Hosea. Hosea 1:2.
2. Amos. Amos 7:15.
3. Ezekiel. Ezekiel 37:1–4.
4. Jonah. Jonah 1:17; 2:10.
5. Joel. Joel 2:28–32.
6. Micah. Micah 5:2.
7. Hosea. Hosea 1:6.
8. Amos. Amos 7:17.
9. Ezekiel. Ezekiel 37:12–14.
10. Jonah. Jonah 3:2–3, 10; 4:1.

26: THE TEMPLE AT JERUSALEM

1. Solomon. 1 Kings 5:5.
2. Hiram. 1 Kings 5:6–9, 18.
3. The most holy place. 1 Kings 8:6.
4. Josiah. 2 Kings 23:23.

5. Nebuchadnezzar. Jeremiah 28:3.
6. Haggai and Zechariah. Ezra 5:1–2.
7. Zerubbabel's. Zechariah 4:9.
8. The second. Matthew 4:3–11.
9. Moneychangers. Matthew 21:12.
10. Jesus. Matthew 24:1–2.

27: JEWELS OF WISDOM
1. Job. Job 1:21.
2. "Is no God." Psalm 14:1.
3. Proverbs. Proverbs 3:6.
4. "Bring it to pass." Psalm 37:5.
5. Ecclesiastes. Ecclesiastes 11:1.
6. "Great riches." Proverbs 22:1.
7. "House of the LORD." Psalm 122:1.
8. You don't know what a day will bring. Proverbs 27:1.
9. "Is not wise." Proverbs 20:1.
10. Solomon. Ecclesiastes 12:1.

28: BIBLE CURIOSITIES
1. A rib. Genesis 2:22.
2. A fish's mouth. Matthew 17:27.
3. A shoe. Ruth 4:6–7.
4. King David. 2 Samuel 6:14–15.
5. Into a herd of swine. Luke 8:33.
6. Solomon. 1 Kings 3:25–27.
7. Elijah. 2 Kings 2:11.
8. Wash seven times in the Jordan River. 2 Kings 5:10.
9. Joash. 2 Kings 11:2–3.
10. Eutychus. Acts 20:9–12.

29: INFAMOUS FAILURES
1. Adam and Eve. Genesis 3:16–19, 23.
2. Jephthah. Judges 11:30–31, 34–36.
3. Herod (many scholars believe this was Herod Agrippa I). Acts 12:21–23.
4. The Philistines. 1 Samuel 5:11–6:1.

5. Samuel. 1 Samuel 8:4–5.
6. Saul. 1 Samuel 15:26.
7. Nabal. 1 Samuel 25:9–10, 37–38.
8. Ananias and Sapphira. Acts 5:1–10.
9. Sceva. Acts 19:13–16.
10. "I have sinned in that I have betrayed the innocent blood." Matthew 27:3–4.

30: PALTRY EXCUSES

1. "The woman whom thou gavest. . .me, she gave me of the tree, and I did eat." Genesis 3:12.
2. "The serpent beguiled me, and I did eat." Genesis 3:13.
3. The people said, "Make us gods" for we don't know what happened to Moses. Exodus 32:23.
4. It isn't customary in our country to give the younger before the firstborn. Genesis 29:25–26.
5. Giants were seen in the land that made us look like grasshoppers. Numbers 13:33.
6. They feared the Jews would put them out of the synagogue. John 9:21–22.
7. "Follow me; and let the dead bury their dead." Matthew 8:21–22.
8. One bought ground and must see it; the other bought oxen and must approve them. Luke 14:18–19.
9. "I have married a wife, and therefore I cannot come." Luke 14:20.
10. He was rich and unwilling to sacrifice to have treasure in heaven. Luke 18:23.

31: PAINFUL PUNISHMENTS

1. Banishment to till the ground. Genesis 3:23–24.
2. Cain. Genesis 4:11, 13.
3. Simeon and Levi. Genesis 34:4–5, 25–27.
4. Lot's wife. Genesis 19:23, 26.
5. Korah. Numbers 16:1–2, 32–33.
6. Aaron's. Leviticus 10:1–2.
7. Moses and Aaron. Numbers 20:12–13.

8. He withheld spoils of war. Joshua 6:26; 7:1, 25.
9. Ark of the covenant. 2 Samuel 6:6–7.
10. Being stoned to death. Leviticus 24:16.

32: PRAYERS THAT PREVAILED
1. Righteous. James 5:16.
2. Samuel. 1 Samuel 1:19–20, 27.
3. Wisdom/an understanding heart. 1 Kings 3:9, 12.
4. Prophets of Baal. 1 Kings 18:19, 36–40.
5. Moses. Exodus 15:23–25.
6. Zacharias. Luke 1:13, 36.
7. "Come forth." John 11:41–44.
8. Pentecost. Acts 1:13–14; 2:1, 4.
9. "They know not what they do." Luke 23:34.
10. The publican/tax collector. Luke 18:13–14.

33: OBSERVING THE SABBATH
1. Creation was completed, and God rested on that day. Genesis 2:3.
2. They gathered twice as much the previous day. Exodus 16:22–23.
3. "Keep it holy." Exodus 20:8.
4. He was stoned to death. Numbers 15:32–36.
5. He taught in the synagogue. Mark 6:2.
6. "Lord also of the Sabbath." Mark 2:23, 27–28.
7. Lawful, Sabbath days. Matthew 12:10–13.
8. Because he watered work animals on the Sabbath, but denied relief to a suffering woman. Luke 13:10–16.
9. The resurrection of Christ. John 20:1, 19.
10. Corinth. 1 Corinthians 16:1–2.

34: GUIDANCE ON GIVING
1. One-tenth/the tithe. Leviticus 27:30, 32.
2. By not giving tithes and offerings. Malachi 3:8.
3. God will open the windows of heaven and pour out abundant blessings. Malachi 3:10.
4. David. 1 Chronicles 29:10, 14.

5. "She. . .cast in all that she had." Mark 12:44.
6. They first gave themselves. 2 Corinthians 8:5.
7. "Loveth a cheerful giver." 2 Corinthians 9:7.
8. They lied to the Holy Spirit about property sold and money given to the church. Acts 5:1–10.
9. Everyone should put aside money each Sunday in relation to earnings. 1 Corinthians 16:1–2.
10. "It shall be given unto you." Luke 6:38.

35: THE BIBLE ON THE BIBLE

1. "Light." Psalm 119:105.
2. Timothy. 2 Timothy 3:15.
3. "It is written." Matthew 4:4, 7, 10.
4. "The sword of the Spirit." Ephesians 6:17.
5. They testify of Him. John 5:39.
6. "By the Holy Ghost." 2 Peter 1:21.
7. Berea. Acts 17:10–11.
8. "Inspiration. . .profitable." 2 Timothy 3:16.
9. Isaiah 53. Acts 8:30, 32.
10. Hebrews 4:12.

36: ANIMALS OF THE BIBLE

1. Animal skins. Genesis 3:21.
2. A ram. Genesis 22:13.
3. An ass/a donkey. Numbers 22:27–28.
4. Hart/deer. Psalm 42:1.
5. a. A donkey. John 12:14–15.
6. A lion. Proverbs 30:30.
7. Foxes. Judges 15:4.
8. Female bears. 2 Kings 2:24.
9. Evil workers who insisted on circumcision for Gentiles. Philippians 3:2.
10. "Lamb. . .blemish." 1 Peter 1:19.

37: HEROIC WOMEN

1. Hebrew midwives. Exodus 1:15–17.
2. Abigail. 1 Samuel 25:18–19, 26–27.

BIBLE IQ

3. Esther. Esther 7:3–4.
4. Jael. Judges 4:17, 21.
5. Ruth. Ruth 1:15–17.
6. Rahab. Joshua 2:1, 4.
7. Jehosheba. 2 Kings 11:1–3.
8. Zarephath. 1 Kings 17:9, 12, 15.
9. Mary Magdalene. John 20:1.
10. Lydia. Acts 16:14–15, 40.

38: A Savior Is Born
1. Caesar Augustus. Luke 2:1.
2. Isaiah. Isaiah 7:14.
3. Micah. Micah 5:2.
4. There was no room in the inn. Luke 2:7.
5. An angel. Luke 2:9–10.
6. A babe would be wrapped in "swaddling clothes"/cloths and lying in a manger. Luke 2:12.
7. "Christ the Lord." Luke 2:11.
8. A star went before them and settled over the child's location. Matthew 2:9.
9. Gold, frankincense, and myrrh. Matthew 2:11.
10. "God with us." Matthew 1:23.

39: From Bethlehem to the River Jordan
1. Either two turtledoves or two young pigeons. Luke 2:24.
2. The Messiah/Christ. Luke 2:25–29.
3. Egypt. Matthew 2:14.
4. Kill all males two and under. Matthew 2:16.
5. Nazareth. Luke 2:39.
6. In the temple with the teachers. Luke 2:46.
7. "God and man." Luke 2:52.
8. "Suffer it to be so now. . .it becometh us to fulfil all righteousness." Matthew 3:15.
9. A descending dove alighted on Him. Matthew 3:16.
10. "This is my beloved Son, in whom I am well pleased." Matthew 3:17.

40: FORERUNNER FOR THE KING

1. Isaiah. Isaiah 40:3; Matthew 3:3.
2. Zacharias and Elisabeth. Luke 1:13.
3. "Is at hand." Matthew 3:1–2.
4. "I have need to be baptized of thee, and comest thou to me?" Matthew 3:14.
5. "Sent before Him." John 3:28.
6. He had told Herod it was unlawful for him to marry his brother's wife. Mark 6:17–18.
7. "Art thou he that should come, or do we look for another?" Matthew 11:2–3.
8. The head of John the Baptist on a charger/platter. Matthew 14:6–8.
9. "Greater than John the Baptist." Matthew 11:11.
10. "Must decrease." John 3:30.

41: JESUS' TEMPTATIONS AND OURS

1. He had fasted forty days and nights. Matthew 4:2–3.
2. "Man shall not live by bread alone, but by every word that proceedeth out of the mouth of God." Matthew 4:3–4.
3. "Thou shalt not tempt the Lord thy God." Matthew 4:7.
4. To worship Satan. Matthew 4:8–9.
5. Angels. Matthew 4:11.
6. "Watch and pray." Matthew 26:41.
7. Above that he is able. 1 Corinthians 10:13.
8. "Deliver us from evil." Matthew 6:13.
9. "Out of temptations." 2 Peter 2:9.
10. The crown of life. James 1:12.

42: BLESSED BEATITUDES

1. Poor in spirit. Matthew 5:3.
2. "Shall be comforted." Matthew 5:4.
3. The meek/humble. Matthew 5:5.
4. "Be filled." Matthew 5:6.
5. "Pure in heart." Matthew 5:8.
6. The peacemakers. Matthew 5:9.
7. They will have a great reward in heaven. Matthew 5:12.

8. Happy (blessed). Psalm 127:3, 5.
9. "If ye do them." John 13:17.
10. "For righteousness' sake." 1 Peter 3:14.

43: THE CHRISTIAN'S EXAMPLE

1. Jesus. Matthew 5:1, 13.
2. "Cannot be hid." Matthew 5:14.
3. So others may see their good works and glorify the Father. Matthew 5:16.
4. Stumble/fall. Romans 14:21.
5. "Foolish men." 1 Peter 2:15.
6. Paul. 1 Corinthians 11:1 (NIV).
7. Peter. 1 Peter 3:1.
8. "And follow me." Matthew 16:24.
9. Timothy. 1 Timothy 4:12.
10. "To teach others also." 2 Timothy 2:2

44: FULFILLING GOD'S LAW

1. Two tablets of stone. Deuteronomy 4:13.
2. In the ark of the covenant. Deuteronomy 31:9, 26.
3. Serve idols. 2 Kings 17:12, 16–18.
4. Paul. Romans 3:19–20.
5. Destroy, fulfill it. Matthew 5:17.
6. Anger, lustful. Matthew 5:21–24, 27–28.
7. Love God supremely and love neighbor as self. Matthew 22:37–40.
8. Love. Romans 13:8, 10.
9. Paul. Galatians 3:24.
10. "That ye love one another; as I have loved you." John 13:34.

45: HOW TO TREAT ENEMIES

1. Mephibosheth. 2 Samuel 9:6–7.
2. "Fear not: for am I in the place of God?" Genesis 50:15, 19–20.
3. Leave your gift until you have made peace with your brother. Matthew 5:23–24.

4. "Death of his Son." Romans 5:10.
5. "Love your enemies, bless them that curse you." Matthew 5:43–44.
6. "Father, forgive them." Luke 23:34.
7. "Lord, lay not this sin to their charge." Acts 7:60.
8. Vengeance belongs to the Lord. Romans 12:19.
9. "Also forgive you." Matthew 6:14.
10. "Whom he may devour." 1 Peter 5:8.

46: HOW TO PRAY
1. "Will not hear me." Psalm 66:18.
2. The Father will reward them openly. Matthew 6:6.
3. The Father knows what we need before we ask. Matthew 6:7–8.
4. "And it shall be opened unto you." Matthew 7:7.
5. He prayed all night on a mountain. Luke 6:12–13.
6. Sleeping. Matthew 26:36–40.
7. "That they might be saved." Romans 10:1.
8. "Requests be made known." Philippians 4:6.
9. Ask God in faith. James 1:5–6.
10. "According to his will." 1 John 5:14.

47: PURSUING RICHES IN HEAVEN
1. "Than great riches." Proverbs 22:1.
2. They are subject to corruption and thievery. Matthew 6:19.
3. "Heart be also." Matthew 6:21.
4. "True riches." Luke 16:11.
5. That he sell what he had and give it to the poor. Mark 10:21.
6. He built larger barns and was not right with God. Luke 12:18–21.
7. Timothy. 1 Timothy 6:17.
8. "Riches in glory." Philippians 4:19.
9. He sold all he had and bought it. Matthew 13:45–46.
10. "All these things." Matthew 6:33.

48. JESUS AND HIS APOSTLES
1. Andrew. John 1:40–41.
2. Peter, James, and John. Mark 5:37.
3. Andrew. John 1:35–40.
4. Matthew/Levi. Matthew 9:9.
5. James and John. Matthew 4:21–22.
6. Simon Peter. Matthew 16:18–19.
7. Nathanael. John 1:47.
8. A potter's field/burial place for strangers. Matthew 27:5–7.
9. Matthias. Acts 1:16, 26.
10. John. John 19:26–27.

49. JESUS AND SPECIAL FRIENDS
1. Lazarus. John 12:1–2.
2. Joseph of Arimathea. Matthew 27:57–60.
3. Simon of Cyrene. Matthew 27:32.
4. Nicodemus. John 3; 19:39–40.
5. Zacchaeus. Luke 19:1–5.
6. The woman at the well. John 4:7, 10.
7. Mary Magdalene. Luke 8:1–2.
8. Mary. John 12:1–3.
9. Martha. John 11:20–22.
10. James and John's. Matthew 20:20–21.

50. JESUS AND THE CHILDREN
1. "As little children." Matthew 18:3.
2. c. Drowning. Matthew 18:6.
3. Cana of Galilee. John 4:46–47, 50.
4. The disciples scolded them. Matthew 19:13.
5. They laughed scornfully. Mark 5:39–40.
6. "Hosanna to the son of David." Matthew 21:15.
7. "Holy Spirit." Luke 11:13.
8. Marketplace. Luke 7:31–32.
9. "That ye love one another; as I have loved you." John 13:33–34.
10. Greatest. Matthew 18:4.

51: WOMEN WHO FOLLOWED JESUS

1. Mary, his mother; Mary Magdalene; Mary, wife of Cleophas. John 19:25.
2. Two mites/a farthing. Mark 12:41–42.
3. She anointed Him for burial. John 12:3–5, 7.
4. "Go, and sin no more." John 8:11.
5. She touched His clothes. Mark 5:28–29.
6. Anna. Luke 2:36–38.
7. Out of their substance/out of their own means. Luke 8:2–3.
8. Simon Peter's. Luke 4:38–39.
9. "Yet the dogs under the table eat of the children's crumbs." Mark 7:27–29.
10. Living water. John 4:5, 7–10.

52: JESUS, THE MIRACLE WORKER

1. Turning water into wine. John 2:1–11.
2. They marvelled, saying, "Even the winds and the sea obey him!" Matthew 8:26–27.
3. A nobleman's son. John 4:46, 50–53.
4. He was carrying his bed on the Sabbath. John 5:8–10.
5. He fell at Jesus' knees, saying, "Depart from me; for I am a sinful man." Luke 5:4–8.
6. "Go shew yourselves unto the priests." Luke 17:12–14.
7. "Woman, thou art loosed from thine infirmity." Luke 13:11–13.
8. "Be not afraid, only believe." Mark 5:35–36.
9. They were afraid, thinking He was a ghost. Matthew 14:25–26.
10. "Jesus, thou son of David, have mercy on me." Mark 10:46–47.

53: FEEDING THE MULTITUDES

1. Send the people away to buy food for themselves. Matthew 14:15.
2. They don't have to leave. You give them something to eat. Matthew 14:16.

3. Five loaves and two fishes. Matthew 14:17.
4. He gave thanks. Matthew 14:19.
5. Twelve. Matthew 14:20.
6. About five thousand. Matthew 14:21.
7. "I will not send them away fasting, lest they faint." Matthew 15:32.
8. Sit down on the ground. Matthew 15:35.
9. Four thousand. Matthew 15:38.
10. "Shall never hunger." John 6:35.

54: THE DIVINE SHEPHERD

1. "Not want." Psalm 23:1.
2. "For thou art with me; thy rod and thy staff they comfort me." Psalm 23:4.
3. "Presence of mine enemies." Psalm 23:5.
4. "Goodness and mercy." Psalm 23:6.
5. "I will dwell in the house of the LORD for ever." Psalm 23:6.
6. Jesus. John 10:11.
7. "A thief and a robber." John 10:1.
8. "Shepherd of the sheep." John 10:2.
9. "They follow me." John 10:27.
10. Peter. 1 Peter 5:4.

55: FAILING THE FRUIT TEST

1. "Leadeth to destruction." Matthew 7:13.
2. "Ravening wolves." Matthew 7:15.
3. A good tree produces good fruit; a corrupt tree produces evil fruit. Matthew 7:17.
4. It will be hewn down and cast into the fire. Matthew 7:19.
5. "The will of my Father." Matthew 7:21.
6. "I never knew you; depart from me, ye that work iniquity." Matthew 7:23.
7. One who hears and obeys Christ's sayings. Matthew 7:24.
8. "Good things." Matthew 12:35.

9. It withered away. Matthew 21:18–19.
10. Have no fellowship with them; rather, reprove them. Ephesians 5:11.

56: MARRIAGE AND DIVORCE

1. God. Genesis 2:18, 24.
2. He was allowed to stay home one year without business or military obligations. Deuteronomy 24:5.
3. "Man put asunder." Matthew 19:6.
4. Cana of Galilee. John 2:1–3.
5. "Gave himself for it." Ephesians 5:25.
6. So their conduct would lead their husbands to believe in God. 1 Peter 3:1.
7. Because of the hardness of their hearts. Matthew 19:7–8.
8. Fornication/adultery. Matthew 19:9.
9. Hebrews. Hebrews 13:4 (NKJV).
10. Reverence/respect her husband. Ephesians 5:33.

57: GREATNESS IN THE KINGDOM

1. Their mother. Matthew 20:20–21.
2. "Ye know not what ye ask." Matthew 20:22.
3. The Father. Matthew 20:23.
4. c. Indignant. Matthew 20:24.
5. Your minister/servant. Matthew 20:26.
6. "Ransom for many." Matthew 20:28.
7. The servant. Luke 22:27.
8. Whoever obeys Christ's commandments and teaches others to obey. Matthew 5:19.
9. He resisted: "Thou shalt never wash my feet." John 13:5, 8.
10. "Wash one another's feet." John 13:14.

58: POINTS FROM PARABLES

1. His disciples would understand, while unbelievers would hear and not understand. Mark 4:11–12.
2. God's Word/message. Mark 4:14.

3. "Rejoice with me; for I have found my sheep which was lost." Luke 15:6.
4. Sold all he had to buy the field. Matthew 13:44.
5. Old wineskins break and the wine runs out. Matthew 9:17(NKJV).
6. Those who hear His sayings and obey them. Matthew 7:24.
7. They were given the same pay as those hired later in the day. Matthew 20:10–13.
8. He did not invest his single pound because of fear. Luke 19:21–24.
9. "Inasmuch as ye have done it unto one of the least of. . . my brethren, ye have done it unto me." Matthew 25:40.
10. Abraham's bosom. Luke 16:22.

59: THE PRODIGAL AND HIS FAMILY

1. Pharisees, scribes. Luke 15:2.
2. In sinful/riotous living. Luke 15:13.
3. Feeding swine. Luke 15:15.
4. Go to his father. Luke 15:17–18.
5. b. Compassionate. Luke 15:20.
6. "Father, I have sinned." Luke 15:21.
7. A robe, ring, and shoes. Luke 15:22.
8. a. Angry. Luke 15:25, 28.
9. "Son, thou art ever with me, and all that I have is thine." Luke 15:31.
10. His lost son had been found alive. Luke 15:32.

60: THE SAMARITAN AND THE WOUNDED TRAVELER

1. "Inherit eternal life." Luke 10:25.
2. "And who is my neighbour?" Luke 10:29.
3. Almost naked and "half dead." Luke 10:30.
4. A priest. Luke 10:31.
5. Looked at him and passed by on the other side. Luke 10:32.
6. c. Compassion. Luke 10:33.

7. The Samaritan bound up his wounds, after treating them with oil and wine. Luke 10:34.
8. To an inn. Luke 10:34.
9. Take care of him and when I return, I'll repay you. Luke 10:35.
10. "Go, and do thou likewise." Luke 10:37.

61: NICODEMUS MEETS JESUS

1. He was a Pharisee and ruler among the Jews. John 3:1.
2. He called Him a teacher of God attested to by miracles. John 3:2.
3. "The kingdom of God." John 3:3.
4. "How can a man be born when he is old?" John 3:4.
5. The wind. John 3:8.
6. "Son of man." John 3:14.
7. "Might be saved." John 3:17.
8. "Light is come into the world, and men loved darkness rather than light." John 3:19.
9. "Doth our law judge any man, before it hear him?" John 7:50–51.
10. He brought spices to anoint Christ's body. John 19:39–40.

62: ZACCHAEUS FINDS JESUS

1. Chief of the publicans/tax collectors. Luke 19:2.
2. He was small of stature, and the crowd pressed close around him. Luke 19:3.
3. "Abide at thy house." Luke 19:5.
4. Jericho. Luke 19:1.
5. He came down hastily and received Him joyfully. Luke 19:6.
6. They murmured that Jesus was dining with a sinner. Luke 19:7.
7. Give them half his wealth. Luke 19:8.
8. He would restore it fourfold. Luke 19:8.
9. Salvation has come to this house today. Luke 19:9.
10. "That which was lost"/the lost. Luke 19:10.

63: JESUS AND THE WOMAN AT THE WELL
1. Galilee. John 4:3–4.
2. Sychar. John 4:5–7.
3. "Give me to drink." John 4:7.
4. He was a Jew; she was a Samaritan. John 4:9.
5. "Shall never thirst." John 4:14.
6. Five. John 4:18.
7. On this mountain in Samaria. John 4:20.
8. "Such to worship him." John 4:23.
9. "Come, see a man, which told me all things that ever I did: is not this the Christ?" John 4:29.
10. Many believed on Christ. John 4:39.

64: FROM PALM SUNDAY TO CALVARY
1. He wept over it. Luke 19:41.
2. "Den of thieves." Mark 11:17.
3. Was the baptism of John from heaven or from men? Mark 11:28–30.
4. "The Lord's death till he come." 1 Corinthians 11:26.
5. "Watch and pray, that ye enter not into temptation." Matthew 26:41.
6. Judas led them to Jesus. John 18:2–3, 5.
7. Cut off the ear of the high priest's servant. John 18:10.
8. That He was able to destroy the temple and rebuild it in three days. Matthew 26:60–61.
9. "I am innocent of the blood of this just person." Matthew 27:24.
10. They put a purple robe and crown of thorns on Him, hailing Him as "King of the Jews." Mark 15:16–18.

65: ANATOMY OF A TRAITOR
1. Judas Iscariot. Matthew 10:4; Mark 3:19.
2. Treasurer. John 13:29.
3. "Was the traitor"/betrayed Him. Luke 6:16.
4. Why wasn't the ointment sold and the money given to the poor? John 12:4–5.
5. The chief priests. Matthew 26:14.

241

6. Thirty pieces of silver. Matthew 26:15.
7. "That thou doest, do quickly." John 13:26–27.
8. With a kiss. Mark 14:44–45.
9. He left and hanged himself. Matthew 27:5.
10. "Had not been born." Matthew 26:24.

66: FROM TRAGEDY TO TRIUMPH

1. Wine with myrrh/gall. Mark 15:23.
2. "THE KING OF THE JEWS." Mark 15:26.
3. "Remember me when thou comest into thy kingdom." Luke 23:42.
4. "Behold thy mother!" John 19:27.
5. Darkness came over the land. Matthew 27:45.
6. "Father, into thy hands I commend my spirit." Luke 23:46.
7. The veil of the temple was torn in two from top to bottom. Matthew 27:50–51.
8. Joseph of Arimathea and Nicodemus. John 19:38–41.
9. An angel of the Lord. Matthew 28:2.
10. She told them she had seen the Lord. John 20:18.

67: CHRIST'S RESURRECTION AND OURS

1. Place his hands in the nail prints. John 20:27.
2. "Above five hundred." 1 Corinthians 15:6.
3. Be raised up. John 6:40.
4. Corinth. 2 Corinthians 4:14.
5. "Your faith." 1 Corinthians 15:14.
6. "The firstfruits." 1 Corinthians 15:20.
7. Death. 1 Corinthians 15:26.
8. "Be changed." 1 Corinthians 15:51.
9. Sin. 1 Corinthians 15:56.
10. "The dead in Christ." 1 Thessalonians 4:16.

68: JESUS' ASCENSION AND INTERCESSION

1. Jerusalem, all Judea, Samaria, and the uttermost part of the earth. Acts 1:8.
2. Forty. Acts 1:3.

3. Two men dressed in white. Acts 1:9–11.
4. Near Bethany. Luke 24:50–51.
5. c. Joyous. Luke 24:52.
6. Lifted them up and blessed the disciples. Luke 24:50.
7. A repentant thief. Luke 23:40–43.
8. "The evil"/"the evil one" (NKJV). John 17:15.
9. "Make intercession." Hebrews 7:25.
10. Hebrews. Hebrews 4:14.

69: WHEN THE POWER FELL AT PENTECOST
1. "Upon all flesh." Joel 2:28.
2. Tarry in Jerusalem until the power falls. Luke 24:49.
3. "Uttermost part of the earth." Acts 1:8.
4. The sound of a "rushing mighty wind" from heaven. Acts 2:2.
5. They spoke in "other tongues." Acts 2:4.
6. Each heard the Gospel in his own language. Acts 2:7–8.
7. They said these men were drunk on "new wine." Acts 2:13.
8. "Lord and Christ." Acts 2:36.
9. "Repent, and be baptized every one of you in the name of Jesus Christ." Acts 2:38.
10. "About three thousand souls." Acts 2:41.

70: WITNESSES SCATTERED ABROAD
1. To the temple. Acts 5:19–21.
2. "God rather than men." Acts 5:29.
3. Gamaliel. Acts 5:34, 38–39.
4. Stephen. Acts 6:5, 8.
5. That he spoke blasphemous words against the temple and Mosaic Law. Acts 6:13.
6. "Lord, lay not this sin to their charge." Acts 7:60.
7. "Preaching the word." Acts 8:4.
8. Philip. Acts 6:5; 8:5.
9. He was directed by an angel to do so. Acts 8:26.
10. To be baptized. Acts 8:35–37.

BIBLE IQ

71: SIMON PETER: A PEBBLE WHO BECAME A ROCK

1. Andrew. John 1:40–42.
2. "The living God." Matthew 16:16.
3. Strengthen the brethren. Luke 22:31–32.
4. He wept bitterly. Luke 22:60–62.
5. "Lovest thou me more than these?" John 21:15.
6. Joel. Acts 2:15–17.
7. "Silver and gold have I none; but such as I have give I thee: In the name of Jesus Christ of Nazareth rise up and walk." Acts 3:6.
8. Dorcas/Tabitha. Acts 9:36–37, 40.
9. The house of Mary, mother of John Mark. Acts 12:11–12.
10. Cephas, meaning "a stone/rock." John 1:42.

72: SAUL: FROM PERSECUTOR TO APOSTLE

1. Stephen. Acts 7:58–59; 8:1.
2. For synagogues in Damascus. Acts 9:1–2.
3. Fell to the ground. Acts 9:3–4.
4. "Saul, Saul, why persecutest thou me?" Acts 9:4.
5. "Arise, and go into the city, and it shall be told thee what thou must do." Acts 9:6.
6. He was stricken blind. Acts 9:8.
7. Ananias. Acts 9:10–11.
8. "Go thy way: for he is a chosen vessel unto me." Acts 9:15.
9. To the synagogues. Acts 9:18–20.
10. They tried to kill him. Acts 9:23.

73: PAUL'S MISSIONARY JOURNEYS

1. They were afraid of him. Acts 9:26.
2. "Antioch." Acts 11:26.
3. They fasted, prayed, and laid their hands on them. Acts 13:1–3.
4. Bar-jesus/Elymas. Acts 13:6, 8–11.
5. The healing of a crippled man. Acts 14:8–12.

6. "Come over into Macedonia, and help us." Acts 16:9.
7. "Sirs, what must I do to be saved?" Acts 16:29–30.
8. They were forbidden by the Holy Spirit. Acts 16:1–3, 6–7.
9. There are no gods made with hands. Acts 19:26.
10. "Unto the Gentiles." Acts 22:17, 21.

74: PAUL'S MISSIONARY COMPANIONS
1. Barnabas. Acts 9:27–28.
2. John Mark. Acts 15:37–39.
3. Timothy. Acts 16:1.
4. Silas. Acts 16:19, 23.
5. Aquila and Priscilla. Acts 18:2–3.
6. Luke. Acts 1:1; 16:10; Luke 1:3.
7. Apollos. Acts 18:24.
8. Epaphroditus. Philippians 4:18.
9. Timothy. 2 Timothy 4:21.
10. Titus. 2 Corinthians 8:23.

75: THE NAME ABOVE ALL NAMES
1. "Every name." Philippians 2:9.
2. Prince of Peace. Isaiah 9:6; Ephesians 2:14.
3. Son of man. Matthew 8:20.
4. Hebrews. Hebrews 12:2.
5. My beloved Son. Matthew 3:17.
6. Bread of life. John 6:10, 35.
7. Light of the world. John 9:4–5.
8. b. Our passover. 1 Corinthians 5:7.
9. The resurrection and the life. John 11:25.
10. "Beginning and the end." Revelation 21:6.

76: PAUL'S VIEWS ON JOY AND SUFFERING
1. "Rejoice," "weep." Romans 12:15.
2. "I am ready not to be bound only, but also to die at Jerusalem for the name of the Lord Jesus." Acts 21:10–13.

3. "Suffer for His sake." Philippians 1:29 (NKJV).
4. He was buffeted by Satan lest he become too proud. 2 Corinthians 12:7.
5. "Made known to God." Philippians 4:6 (NKJV).
6. Timothy. 2 Timothy 1:3–4 (NKJV).
7. That we may comfort others in trouble. 2 Corinthians 1:4.
8. Colosse. Colossians 1:24 (NKJV).
9. Much greater eternal glory. 2 Corinthians 4:17.
10. "Reign with him." 2 Timothy 2:12.

77: Christ and His Church

1. "The gates of hell shall not prevail against it." Matthew 16:18.
2. Paul. Ephesians 2:20.
3. "Church," "preeminence." Colossians 1:18.
4. Ephesians. Ephesians 5:30.
5. Peter. 1 Peter 2:5.
6. "One of another"/"of one another" (NKJV). Romans 12:5.
7. The Ephesian elders. Acts 20:17, 28.
8. c. Perfect the saints/edify the body. Ephesians 4:11–12.
9. The coming of the Lord was near. Hebrews 10:25.
10. b. Holy and blameless. Ephesians 5:27.

78: On Guard for Christ's Return

1. "In all the world." Matthew 24:14.
2. The Father. Matthew 24:36.
3. His angels. Matthew 24:31.
4. "Your Lord doth come." Matthew 24:42.
5. They had no oil in their lamps. Matthew 25:8–10.
6. "Inasmuch as ye did it not to one of the least of these, ye did it not to me." Matthew 25:45.
7. To ones fashioned like His glorious body. Philippians 3:20–21.
8. According to their works. Matthew 16:27.
9. He raised Him from the dead. Acts 17:31.

10. "Receive you unto myself." John 14:3.

79: COUNSEL FOR YOUNG MINISTERS
1. Timothy. 2 Timothy 2:3.
2. Titus. Titus 1:5.
3. "The word of truth." 2 Timothy 2:15.
4. The time will come when sound doctrine will not be endured. 2 Timothy 4:2–3.
5. "Evangelist," "ministry." 2 Timothy 4:5.
6. "Persecution." 2 Timothy 3:12.
7. "Love of money." 1 Timothy 6:10.
8. "Living God." 1 Timothy 6:17.
9. Titus. Titus 1:4.
10. "Nothing is pure." Titus 1:15 (NKJV).

80: ACCEPTING GENTILES AS BROTHERS
1. Isaiah. Isaiah 60:3–5.
2. Cornelius. Acts 10:1–5.
3. Praying on the housetop. Acts 10:9.
4. "Rise, Peter; kill, and eat." Acts 10:10–13.
5. "Not so, Lord; for I have never eaten any thing that is common or unclean." Acts 10:14.
6. "Common"/unclean. Acts 10:15.
7. He fell at his feet and bowed before him. Acts 10:25.
8. The Holy Spirit fell on the Gentiles. Acts 10:44–45.
9. Circumcised. Acts 15:24, 28–29.
10. Christ, by His death on the cross. Ephesians 2:14–16.

81: GIFTS FROM THE HOLY SPIRIT
1. The gift of the Holy Spirit. Acts 2:38.
2. "Children of God." Romans 8:16.
3. Ephesus. Ephesians 4:30.
4. "Come to you." John 14:18.
5. John. 1 John 4:1–3.
6. "Grace given us." Romans 12:6 (NIV).
7. b. Simplicity. Romans 12:8.
8. "Proportion of faith." Romans 12:6.

9. Corinth. 1 Corinthians 12:11 (NKJV).
10. Love. 1 Corinthians 12:31; 13:13.

82: LOVE, THE MOST ABIDING VIRTUE

1. "Thou shalt love the Lord thy God with all thy heart, and with all thy soul, and with all thy mind." Matthew 22:37–38.
2. "For his friends." John 15:13.
3. "I have loved you." John 15:12.
4. "World," "Son," "everlasting life." John 3:16.
5. Romans. Romans 13:8.
6. One becomes as "sounding brass, or a tinkling cymbal." 1 Corinthians 13:1.
7. "Profiteth me nothing." 1 Corinthians 13:3.
8. c. Charity/love. 1 Corinthians 13:13.
9. John. 1 John 3:1.
10. "First loved us." 1 John 4:19.

83: COMMITTED TO GOD'S SERVICE

1. The mercies of God. Romans 12:1.
2. By the renewing of their minds. Romans 12:2.
3. "Dwelleth in you." 1 Corinthians 3:16.
4. Corinth. 1 Corinthians 6:20.
5. "Unto holiness." 1 Thessalonians 4:7.
6. "Children of God." Romans 8:16.
7. "Unto the day of redemption." Ephesians 4:30.
8. Ephesus. Ephesians 4:15.
9. Titus. Titus 2:14.
10. "Crooked and perverse nation." Philippians 2:15.

84: OBLIGATION TO A WEAK BROTHER

1. Isaiah 35:3–4 (NKJV).
2. Paul. Acts 20:35 (NKJV).
3. "His brother's way." Romans 14:13.
4. "We. . .that are strong." Romans 15:1.
5. "Save some." 1 Corinthians 9:22 (NKJV).
6. "Edify not." 1 Corinthians 10:23.

7. Eating and drinking in an unworthy manner. 1 Corinthians 11:29–30.
8. Take heed your liberty does not cause the weak to stumble. 1 Corinthians 8:9.
9. They should consider the possibility that they would also be tempted. Galatians 6:1.
10. "Is sufficient for thee." 2 Corinthians 12:7–9.

85: THE CHRISTIAN'S OBLIGATION AS CITIZEN

1. Babylon. Jeremiah 29:1, 7.
2. Because all authority comes from God. Romans 13:1.
3. "Caesar," "God," "God's." Matthew 22:21.
4. "Good," "sword in vain." Romans 13:4 (NKJV).
5. "For conscience sake." Romans 13:5.
6. Timothy. 1 Timothy 2:1–2.
7. Peter. 1 Peter 2:17.
8. They are working for God as they are carrying out their duties. Romans 13:6.
9. Simon Peter. Acts 5:29.
10. Heaven. Philippians 3:20.

86: AMBASSADORS FOR CHRIST

1. Ezekiel. Ezekiel 33:7–8.
2. He'd make them "fishers of men." Matthew 4:19.
3. Pray the Lord of the harvest to send out laborers. Luke 10:1–2.
4. "To every creature." Mark 16:15.
5. "Send I you." John 20:21.
6. Paul. Romans 10:14–15.
7. "All things are become new." 2 Corinthians 5:17.
8. Ministry of reconciliation. 2 Corinthians 5:18–19.
9. Peter and John. Acts 4:19–20.
10. "Be ye reconciled to God." 2 Corinthians 5:20.

87: SALVATION BY GRACE THROUGH FAITH

1. Romans. Romans 5:1–2.
2. "Gift of God." Ephesians 2:8.

3. Lest men should boast. Ephesians 2:9.
4. If so, Christ died in vain. Galatians 2:21.
5. Titus. Titus 3:5.
6. "Sinners to repentance." Matthew 9:13.
7. The Jerusalem council. Acts 15:2, 7, 11.
8. "Everlasting life." John 3:16.
9. "Christ Jesus." Romans 3:24.
10. Peter. 1 Peter 1:5.

88: WORKPLACE ETHICS
1. All He made was "very good." Genesis 1:31.
2. Adam. Genesis 3:19.
3. "With thy might." Ecclesiastes 9:10.
4. "When no man can work." John 9:4.
5. Tentmaking. Acts 18:1–3.
6. "Should he eat." 2 Thessalonians 3:10.
7. "From the heart." Ephesians 6:5–6.
8. The Ephesians. Ephesians 6:9.
9. Paul. Colossians 3:17.
10. Corinth. 1 Corinthians 15:58.

89: FAMILY VALUES FOR CHRISTIANS
1. "Be fruitful, and multiply, and replenish the earth." Genesis 1:28.
2. Long life in the land given by the Lord. Exodus 20:12.
3. A gift dedicated to God. Mark 7:11–13.
4. They have denied the faith and are worse than infidels. 1 Timothy 5:8.
5. "Himself," "reverence"/"respects" (NKJV). Ephesians 5:33.
6. "This is right." Ephesians 6:1.
7. "The nurture and admonition of the Lord." Ephesians 6:4.
8. Timothy. 2 Timothy 1:5.
9. The older women. Titus 2:3–5.
10. "My mother and my brethren are these which hear the word of God, and do it." Luke 8:21.

90: On Guard for Holy Living

1. "I am holy." Leviticus 11:44.
2. Jesus. Luke 9:24.
3. "Wiles of the devil." Ephesians 6:11.
4. The shield of faith. Ephesians 6:16.
5. Paul. Philippians 1:6 (NKJV).
6. Colosse. Colossians 3:17.
7. Thessalonica. 2 Thessalonians 3:3 (NKJV).
8. "Against that day." 2 Timothy 1:12.
9. "True holiness." Ephesians 4:22–24.
10. Titus. Titus 2:12–13.

91: The Lordship of Christ

1. Thomas. John 14:6.
2. "That dwell therein." Psalm 24:1.
3. The Sanhedrin. Acts 4:5–8, 12 (NKJV).
4. He humbled Himself and became obedient unto death. Philippians 2:8–11.
5. Paul. Romans 1:16.
6. Colosse. Colossians 2:9–10 (NKJV).
7. "Over all creation" (NKJV)/"of every creature." Colossians 1:15.
8. Timothy. 1 Timothy 6:15.
9. At His right hand in heaven. Ephesians 1:20, 22.
10. Revelation. Revelation 11:15.

92: Christ's Second Coming

1. Paul. 1 Thessalonians 5:23.
2. With a shout, the voice of the archangel, and the trump of God. 1 Thessalonians 4:16.
3. "The glorious appearing of the great God and our Savior Jesus Christ." Titus 2:13.
4. Peter. 2 Peter 3:9–10 (NKJV).
5. James. James 5:7 (NKJV).
6. "Those who sleep in Jesus." 1 Thessalonians 4:14 (NKJV).
7. They will be caught up to meet the Lord in the air. 1 Thessalonians 4:17.

8. "These shall be punished with everlasting destruction from the presence of the Lord." 2 Thessalonians 1:8–9 (NKJV).
9. "Son of man cometh." Matthew 24:44.
10. "According as his work." Revelation 22:12.

93: RELIGION FOR DAILY LIFE

1. Pray to God. James 1:5.
2. Keeping self unspotted from the world. James 1:27.
3. "Dead." James 2:20.
4. "Ye have not, because ye ask not." James 4:2.
5. We ask amiss, for self-indulgence. James 4:3.
6. Send for church elders to pray and anoint him with oil. James 5:14.
7. Fire from hell. James 3:6.
8. "Guilty of all." James 2:10.
9. "To him it is sin." James 4:17.
10. He saves a soul from death and covers a multitude of sins. James 5:20.

94: GUIDANCE FOR SPIRITUAL GROWTH

1. "Grow thereby." 1 Peter 2:2.
2. That they may grow up into Christ in all things. Ephesians 4:15.
3. "High calling of God." Philippians 3:14.
4. Colosse. Colossians 1:10.
5. "To be content." Philippians 4:11.
6. Hebrews. Hebrews 11:6.
7. Peter. 1 Peter 5:10.
8. "Now and for ever." 2 Peter 3:18.
9. "Exceeding joy." Jude 1:24.
10. Thessalonica. 1 Thessalonians 2:12.

95: CHRIST'S PRIESTHOOD AND OURS

1. "The man Christ Jesus." 1 Timothy 2:5.
2. Come boldly to the throne of grace to find help. Hebrews 4:15–16.

3. By His death/His flesh. Ephesians 2:14–15.
4. Direct access. Matthew 27:50–51; Ephesians 3:11–12.
5. By His own shed blood. Hebrews 9:12–14.
6. Exodus 19:5–6 (NKJV).
7. First Peter. 1 Peter 2:9 (NKJV).
8. John. Revelation 1:5–6 (NKJV).
9. "Be healed." James 5:16 (NKJV).
10. Galatians. Galatians 3:28 (NKJV).

96: SUFFERING AS A CHRISTIAN
1. Jesus. John 16:33.
2. "Kingdom of heaven." Matthew 5:10.
3. They rejoiced that they were worthy to suffer shame for Christ. Acts 5:41.
4. "Patience." Romans 5:3.
5. Not worth comparing with the glory that shall be revealed in us. Romans 8:18.
6. Absolutely nothing. Romans 8:35, 38–39.
7. "Suffer for His sake." Philippians 1:29 (NKJV).
8. Peter. 1 Peter 3:17 (NKJV).
9. "Glorify God." 1 Peter 4:16.
10. Smyrna. Revelation 2:8–10.

97: PRECIOUS PROMISES
1. "Direct thy paths." Proverbs 3:6.
2. "When he is old, he will not depart from it." Proverbs 22:6.
3. Jesus. Matthew 11:28.
4. "Opened unto you." Matthew 7:7.
5. "Whatsoever ye shall ask of the Father in my name, he may give it you." John 15:16.
6. Ecclesiastes. Ecclesiastes 11:1.
7. They would reap in due time if they didn't faint. Galatians 6:9.
8. "Which strengtheneth me." Philippians 4:13.
9. James. James 5:15.
10. "He may exalt you in due time." 1 Peter 5:6.

98: MARKS OF THE BELIEVER
1. They have fellowship with one another. 1 John 1:7.
2. "From all unrighteousness." 1 John 1:9.
3. "A liar, and the truth is not in him." 1 John 2:4.
4. He is in darkness until now. 1 John 2:9.
5. "Love of the Father." 1 John 2:15 (NKJV).
6. "We love the brethren." 1 John 3:14.
7. "Has come in the flesh." 1 John 4:2 (NKJV).
8. Our faith. 1 John 5:4.
9. "First loved us." 1 John 4:19 (NKJV).
10. That you may know you have eternal life and believe in Christ. 1 John 5:13.

99: REVELATION TO SEVEN CHURCHES
1. Patmos, Sunday. Revelation 1:9–10.
2. Asia. Revelation 1:11.
3. "One like the Son of Man." Revelation 1:13 (NKJV).
4. The angels of the seven churches. Revelation 1:20.
5. They had left their "first love." Revelation 2:1, 4.
6. "The synagogue of Satan." Revelation 2:9.
7. Pergamos and Thyatira. Revelation 2:12–14, 18–20.
8. Sardis. Revelation 3:1.
9. Philadelphia. Revelation 3:7–8.
10. They were "lukewarm." Revelation 3:14–16.

100: GLORIOUS NEW JERUSALEM
1. Peter. 1 Peter 1:3–4.
2. Paul. 2 Corinthians 5:1 (NKJV).
3. "Him as he is." 1 John 3:2.
4. Those who came out of "great tribulation." Revelation 7:14–15.
5. They rest from their labors and their works follow them. Revelation 14:13.
6. "As a bride adorned for her husband." Revelation 21:2.
7. "Be their God." Revelation 21:3.

8. "Former things are passed away." Revelation 21:4.
9. "The Lord God Almighty and the Lamb are its temple." Revelation 21:22 (NKJV).
10. The Lamb's Book of Life. Revelation 21:27.

LIKE JOKES OR TRIVIA?

Then check out these great books from Barbour Publishing!